GARDEN
ON TRIAL
Wildlife

GARDEN *Wildlife* ON TRIAL

VERDICTS ON THE GARDEN'S FRIENDS AND FOES

Ruth Binney

RP

RYDON
PUBLISHING

A Rydon Publishing Book
35 The Quadrant
Hassocks
West Sussex
BN6 8BP
www.rydonpublishing.co.uk
www.rydonpublishing.com

First published by Rydon Publishing in 2021
Copyright © Ruth Binney 2021

ISBN: 978-1-910821-29-9

CONTENTS

Introduction

The challenge of creating and tending a garden is like trying to complete a complex jigsaw puzzle. When all the pieces are correctly in place the result is a harmonious whole – an ecosystem in which a wide diversity of plants and animals support each other for their mutual benefit.

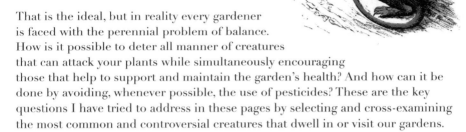

That is the ideal, but in reality every gardener is faced with the perennial problem of balance. How is it possible to deter all manner of creatures that can attack your plants while simultaneously encouraging those that help to support and maintain the garden's health? And how can it be done by avoiding, whenever possible, the use of pesticides? These are the key questions I have tried to address in these pages by selecting and cross-examining the most common and controversial creatures that dwell in or visit our gardens.

Know your neighbours

Essential to managing a garden that is friendly to both wildlife and your plants is to know who you're dealing with. Apart from grey squirrels, a brave rabbit and a deer you might see eating your roses while you have your breakfast, most garden mammals emerge from their hiding places to feed at night, selecting a wide diet ranging from slugs and beetles to the best of your fruit and vegetables. Frogs and toads, too, are chiefly nocturnal. Birds, by contrast (owls are the notable exception) fly in to feed from dawn, retiring to the safety of the garden's vegetation at nightfall. While it is easy enough to tempt them with well-stocked bird feeders and berried shrubs, it is impossible to suppress their appetites for your soft fruit, or for a host of invertebrates, good and bad, including earthworms, leatherjackets and caterpillars of all kinds.

But it is the smallest creatures that present the biggest conundrum. How is it possible to encourage the pollinators and other beneficial insects, and the earthworms that help to cultivate the soil, while keeping at bay the sap-sucking aphids, the destructive carrot flies and voracious slugs and snails? It is in within this invertebrate world that so many of the keys to the garden ecosystem lie, and as well as being able to identify the most important, knowing more about their lifestyles and life cycles is key to creating the balance between the plants and animals that inhabit your plot. And all becomes so much clearer once you know, for example, that aphids are essential foods for the larvae of ladybirds and hoverflies, that lacewings gobble up scale insects and that leatherjackets in the lawn are the magnet for starlings.

A garden plan

Armed with the knowledge of what each member of the garden wildlife community needs for survival, it becomes possible to work out the best ways to plan and maintain your garden. Around the perimeter, hedges of all kinds will be an asset, both as a barrier and as shelter and, ideally, a food source. Fencing may be necessary, depending on your visitors, but exit and entry points may be needed if you have hedgehogs, for example. Trees and shrubs will provide the backbone to the garden and give the added benefits of flowers and fruit.

For the remainder of the garden, plants that attract pollinators are a good place to start, which you can choose with the help of the lists in the reference section. When choosing, remember that single, not double or complex flowers are easiest for most pollinators to visit and that flat-topped umbellifers are essential to support hoverflies. When it comes to flowers and vegetables, all gardeners have their favourites, but it is always wise to look for varieties and cultivars bred for resistance to any particular problems you may have.

Water in the garden, whether a pond or simply a birdbath, can benefit animals of all kinds, whether honeybees that need water for making wax or to prevent hedgehogs from dehydration. The pondside is a haven for frogs and toads – and a perfect resting place for visiting herons that will love to feed on your fish.

Maintaining good health

A well-kept garden will undoubtedly benefit your
garden's ecosystem, preserve biodiversity and protect
the futures of those creatures whose numbers are in
serious decline. While it is important to clear away dead
plants and debris, many creatures will appreciate the
shelter and food source contained in piles of leaves, logs
or long grass, especially in winter. Uncut perennials – and
grasses – can be both a resting place and nesting material. And
when it comes to weeds, it is well worth letting those such as
clover, buttercups and dandelions bloom on your lawn or other
'convenient' garden locations in order to attract pollinators to
the maximum.

The compost heap is also a vital refuge and food source for many invertebrates.
Not only does it help recycle food and garden waste but, when dug into the soil,
compost massively improves its nutrient balance. In the vegetable garden, rotating
crops is often key to countermanding the effects of unwelcome pests such as
wireworm.

There are times, as in the case of a box caterpillar invasion, when you may have
no alternative to digging up plants and replacing them with a pest free alternative.
When all else fails – when you've picked off snails by torchlight, composted
caterpillars and hosed aphids off your roses – then an organic pesticide should be
your first choice but, most important of all, a pesticide, even a mild home-made
version, should never, ever, be used on or near open flowers.

My thanks

As ever my thanks are due to my publisher Robert Ertle, to designer Prudence
Rogers and my editor Verity Graves-Morris. By his own admission he was certainly
no gardener, but my late partner Andrew Fawcett encouraged me in my writing
every day, and I dedicate this book to his memory.

Ruth Binney, Cardiff, 2021

Mammals
and other
Vertebrates

During daylight hours, the only mammals you are likely to see in your garden are grey squirrels bossing birds away from your feeders or scooting up and down trees, or perhaps the occasional hungry wood mouse. It is at dusk that the majority of these residents or visitors come out from their hiding places to hunt for food. In doing so they can be enormously helpful, eating their way through huge quantities of pestiferous insects, slugs and other invertebrates, but also munching vast quantities of worms, eating roses and other prized plants and excavating holes in your lawns, beds and borders.

Satisfying the balance of nature in the garden is crucial for garden mammals. It is perfectly reasonable to put up fencing to deter deer, which can ravage a rose bed overnight, or to keep out marauding rabbits, and to use netting to protect fruit and vegetables from being eaten by foxes, rats and the like. And a clean and tidy garden will discourage scavengers such as foxes, which may well need – certainly in urban circumstances and when there are children in the family – to be prevented from making dens and rearing young in 'cosy' sites such as underneath decking.

What is most important to the garden mammal population is to desist completely, or except in exceptional circumstances, from using pesticides. Not only will these rob creatures of food but can poison them in the process. A healthy, well-cultivated garden will encourage the earthworms on which so many of these creatures depend, usually without depleting the supply significantly. Animals that are welcome visitors also need safe entry and exit points, as well as plenty of good cover for daytime resting and for home making and breeding. Hedges, piles of leaves and patches of long grass left uncut all winter all work to these creatures' advantage. Mammals are afforded protection in law, even species regarded as pests which, if eliminated, must always be handled humanely.

Alongside mammals, the garden is home to frogs, toads and, if you have a pond, to newts as well. Equally susceptible to being killed by pesticides, these amphibians are also indispensible in keeping the quantity of garden slugs, insects and the like in check. Slow worms will add to the army of nature's pest controllers and, with other reptiles such as lizards and grass snakes, are afforded protected status.

BADGERS

European badger *Meles meles*

Family Mustelidae

VERDICT

Badgers can be enormously destructive in their search for food, which includes garden crops as well as a variety of invertebrates. Knowledge and ingenuity are vital in controlling these protected creatures.

FOR THE DEFENCE

Badgers will help to rid the garden of unwanted insect larvae such as leatherjackets and cutworms – but at a cost. And the visit of a badger is a boon to those devoted to badger protection and conservation.

FOR THE PROSECUTION

A badger excavating your garden with its sharp claws can destroy a lawn or compost heap overnight as it searches for food, which will feature earthworms for preference. It will also dig up and eat bulbs and tubers and raid your fruit bushes and vegetable patch. Bee and wasp nests are also vulnerable to raids, while any spilled peanuts from a bird feeder are an irresistible magnet. A badger confronted with a pet dog, cat or guinea pig will almost invariably attack.

THE TREATMENT

Deterrence is the key to keeping the garden badger free. If badgers are causing serious problems, contact The Badger Trust for advice.
• Put up a strong wooden fence at least 1 m (3 ft) high covered with wire mesh that extends 60 cm (2 ft) below ground. Also consider electric fencing.
• Remove potential food sources. Clear up peanuts from under bird feeders and improve the quality of your lawn to minimize its invasion by leatherjackets and the like (see Insects and other Invertebrates). Aeration to improve drainage is key.
• Block off any obvious entrances – badgers are territorial and tend to stick to the same routes.
• Clear any overgrown area that badgers may use to gather bedding material for their setts.
But if you choose to encourage them:
• Within a controlled area, put out peanuts, raisins, soft fruit or bread soaked in water and spread with peanut butter. Never offer meat or dairy foods.

Did you know?

- Badgers are extremely noisy, communicating with barks, grunts and even screams.
- 'Brock' is an Old English word for a badger, and part of many place names such as Brockenhurst and Brockhampton.
- A fully grown male badger can weigh 12 kg (26½ lb).
- Badgers will sometimes eat rabbits, rats, mice and even hedgehogs.
- Tree bark can be damaged as badgers use trunks to sharpen their claws.
- Although they are less active in winter, badgers do not hibernate.

DEER

Fallow deer *Dama dama*

Family Cervidae

VERDICT

Deer can ravage a garden overnight, eating flowers, vegetables, fruit and foliage and stripping away bark. Roe and muntjac deer are the most common offenders.

FOR THE DEFENCE

It is hard not to admire the beauty of these mammals, which appear to be becoming ever bolder in entering gardens singly or even in small groups between dusk and dawn.

FOR THE PROSECUTION

From roses to runner beans, and from holly to hardy geraniums, deer will do their damage over a wide range, stripping off buds, leaves and stems and typically leaving ragged, shredded remains (unlike rabbits that make clean cuts). Young plants are most at risk. Fruits are their favourite food in the autumn while bark provides them with sustenance in winter. In summer, male deer will also fray tree bark by rubbing their antlers on it to remove any newly formed 'velvet'.

THE TREATMENT

Deterring deer is difficult but worth trying. Contrary to popular belief, lion dung and bags of human hair stuffed into old tights are generally ineffective repellents.

• Install fencing or netting but make sure it is at least 1.5 m (4½ ft) tall to prevent deer from jumping over it, and check that there are no gaps through which the animals can squeeze. And make sure that it is very well secured at the base. Avoid harmful electric fencing.

• Fit deer-proof gates to garden entrances.

• Plant tall, thick hedges, ideally containing brambles, and if your landscape allows, dig a ditch around the garden exterior.

• Try an ultrasonic siren or flashing lights, but be prepared for only temporary success; deer will quickly learn to ignore them.

• Secure protective plastic tubes around tree trunks of deciduous trees and netting guards around conifers and shrubs.

• Protect delicate tree shoots with sheep's wool twisted around them.

• Keep a dog – deer don't like their barking or smell.

• Use a deterrent spray containing aluminium sulphate.

Planting basics

Choose your plants with care to help avoid problems.

- Deer resistant species include camellias, fuschias, hellebores, hydrangeas, lavender, irises, hostas, poppies and sedums.

- Plants most vulnerable to attack include roses, bluebells, clematis, honeysuckle, lupins and sweet williams.

- Encourage 'weedy' plants that deer like to eat such as yarrow, campions, rowans, rosebay willowherb, cinquefoil, blackberries and rowan.

- For hedging, choose box, cypress or juniper which deer don't like to eat.

- Plant mint, thyme and sage whose aromas will deter deer.

FOXES

European red fox *Vulpes vulpes*

Family Canidae

Efficient, opportunist scavengers that damage plants and feed on fruit. They will eat rabbits, rodents and invertebrates, may breed in the garden, and can be dangerous to humans if treated as pets.

FOR THE DEFENCE

Where rabbits and rodents are a nuisance, foxes can certainly help reduce their prevalence, using their acute sense of smell and keen hearing to detect prey. When in good health foxes are superb looking creatures with bushy tails or brushes. Foxes are the 'stars' of many favourite tales, including:
The Tale of Mr Tod – Beatrix Potter's story of the rivalry between the fox and the badger.
The Fox and the Grapes – Aesop's fable whose moral is that it is easy to despise what you can't obtain.

FOR THE PROSECUTION

In pursuit of food, foxes will trample or dig up plants, and in autumn gorge on ripe or windfall fruit. They can chew through hosepipes and polytunnels and decimate lawns as they root for chafer grubs. Fox lairs (temporary shelters) are commonly made under sheds and in dense vegetation, and earths for breeding are excavated under hedges, in allotments, or even made under decking. As they mark out their territory, foxes leave behind smelly faeces and urine. If fed and encouraged to feel no threat from humans, foxes can even enter houses and attack babies and children.

THE TREATMENT

Deterrence is the key to dealing with foxes, but gardeners need to think well beyond netting and fencing which can be tunnelled under or jumped over.
• Keep the garden tidy – wild areas are great for pollinators but ideal for fox dens and lairs.
• Avoid using bonemeal or other animal-based maunures and composts that will attract foxes.
• Light the garden at night with motion-activated floodlights – foxes do most of their feeding in the hours of darkness.
• Use an ultrasonic scarer, although foxes can learn to tolerate these.
• Make sure there are no gaps in decking through which foxes can enter.
• Put custom made 'fox spikes' on the top of walls, fences and around entry points.
• Install an automatic fox-repellent water pistol.
• Scoop up any faeces and replace them with a repellent.

A foxy name

In Middle English the fox is known as 'tod'. The name Reynard comes from the German *Rennard*.

FROGS

Common frog *Rana temporaria*

Family Ranidae

VERDICT

Always welcome for their pest-eating abilities, frogs need water for egg laying and tadpole development. However they can attract less welcome predators and provoke phobic reactions.

FOR THE DEFENCE

As well as insects such as flies of all kinds, which they catch by shooting out their sticky tongues, adult frogs help to rid the garden of slugs and snails. The tadpoles feed on the green algae that can quickly cloud a pond in spring.

FOR THE PROSECUTION

Frogs in the garden can encourage the attention of crows, herons, rats, foxes and other potentially damaging predators. Severe aversion to frogs – including their croaks – is not uncommon and is known as ranidaphobia.

THE TREATMENT

Help to encourage frogs by:
- **Avoiding synthetic pesticides, including slug pellets and artificial weedkillers.**
- **Providing damp foliage or piles of debris.**
- **Maintaining a healthy pond for breeding with shallow, plant-filled margins.**
- **Using pebbles to make small frog shelters, or placing upturned flowerpots on circles of stones.**
- **In winter, covering a compost heap with a tarpaulin to keep it warm.**

WARNING!
Never move frogspawn from one pond to another. This can encourage the deadly red-leg disease to which frogs are prone.

Would you believe it?

- Because of its croak, hanging a frog in a chimney was once believed to be a cure for whooping cough – as was eating a live frog.

- Meeting a frog is said to confer wealth. In Scotland a prudent housewife would keep one in her cream bowl.

- Frogspawn is an old weather forecaster – when laid near the pond edges it was believed to presage summer storms; when laid in the pond centre, drought was thought most likely.

Froggy facts

- Frogs breathe through their smooth skins, making them particularly prone to contamination with pesticides and glyphosate-based weedkillers.
- They are mainly active at night.
- Young adults spend two years on land before returning to water to mate.
- A single female lays some 2,000 eggs in a mass of spawn about the size of a tennis ball.
- Only 10 percent of tadpoles, at best, will survive to adulthood; they are mostly eaten by dragonfly larvae and water boatmen, but also by newts. Many froglets become bird food.
- A fully grown frog can leap up to 50 cm (20 in).

GREY SQUIRRELS

Family Sciuridae

Eastern grey squirrel *Sciurus carolinensis*

VERDICT

Grey squirrels attack fruit, flowers and vegetables, strip tree bark, eat the eggs of nesting garden birds and devour the contents of simple bird feeders. They are active all year round.

FOR THE DEFENCE

It is hard not to admire the grey squirrel for its agility and adaptability. Because its body can store fat it can survive long periods without food.

FOR THE PROSECUTION

Grey squirrels' favourite foods include sweetcorn, beans and peas, strawberries (even when green), apples, pears, nuts, tulip bulbs, crocus corms and the buds of magnolias and camellias. A crop can be stripped virtually overnight. Favourite tree barks include sycamore, ash, maple and beech. They will dig up a lawn to bury their nuts and can even munch through the plastic of netting and hosepipes.

THE TREATMENT

Shooting and trapping are legal but generally impractical, and it is unlawful to release a trapped squirrel into the wild. Ultimately you will probably have to live and let live but these measures can help:
• Protect vulnerable plants with substantial wire netting. Growing crops in blocks, not rows, makes this much easier to manage.
• Use 'prickle strips' laid on the ground or tied around young tree trunks to deter them.
• Plant bulbs in wire baskets with additional netting on top.
• Invest in squirrel-proof bird feeders.
• Try animal deterrent sprays and ultrasonic 'scarers', although they will usually only work temporarily.

American imports

Grey squirrels were originally introduced to Britain from Eastern USA between 1876 and 1929. By the late 1930s they had already reduced the dainty native red squirrels to rarities by competing with them for food – unlike greys, the reds need to feed constantly on a diet focused on nuts. Reds are also more disease prone.

Weather guides

• It's said that when, in autumn, you see a squirrel eating nuts on a tree (not taking them to store) we should expect a warm winter. In contrast, super-active nut hoarding is a sign of a cold winter to come.
• Squirrels can sense the direction of the prevailing wind and will build their untidy-looking nests (dreys) with their entrances facing in the opposite direction, affording good protection.

HEDGEHOGS

European hedgehog *Erinaceus europaeus*

Family Erinaceidae

VERDICT

Increasingly rare, these unique visitors eat a variety of common invertebrates, from slugs to beetles, but can cause some damage to lawns. Hedgehogs need safe places to shelter and hibernate.

FOR THE DEFENCE

Slugs, snails and caterpillars – and even mice – are among the garden pests eaten by hedgehogs, which are detected largely by scent in the creatures' nocturnal forays. A resident hedgehog is always welcome.

FOR THE PROSECUTION

Hedgehogs consume many creatures valuable to the gardener, including earthworms, frogs and pollinating insects, and can eat birds' eggs. They will defecate on lawns and can transmit the fungal infection ringworm to humans.

THE TREATMENT

Do as much as you can to encourage hedgehogs to survive and thrive in your garden.

• Don't use slug pellets – they will poison the hedgehog's food.

• Provide a shallow bowl of water and, from November to March, when food is scarce but the weather warm, offer pelleted cat food or mealworms for any individual that emerges from hibernation. Never put out milk – hedgehogs are lactose intolerant.

• Leave unkempt areas where hedgehogs can make daytime lairs, and piles of leaves and cut vegetation where they can hibernate.

• If possible, create a 'hedgehog highway' to allow them to roam. A 15 x 15 cm (6 x 6 in) hole in a fence is perfect, or remove the bottom slats from a garden gate.

• Always check for hedgehogs before you light a bonfire and use a strimmer with extreme care.

That's amazing!

- In 1950 the UK hedgehog population was 35 million but by 2015 it had slumped to just 1 million.
- A fully grown hedgehog has about 6,000 spines.
- Hedgehogs grunt loudly, hence their name.
- A badger can unroll a hedgehog with its paws, making the animal screech as it meets its end.
- Hedgehogs groom themselves with a frothy saliva. This may help deal with the fleas that riddle their skins.
- Adults can travel up to 2 km (1¼ miles) in a single night.
- Hedgehogs were once wrongly accused of sucking milk from cows' udders and killed as a result. They have also been condemned as witches in disguise.

BE AWARE!

Only pick up a hedgehog if it is out during the middle of the day. Wear the thickest possible gloves and take it to an animal rescue centre immediately. A hibernating hedgehog can appear to be dead: don't disturb it.

MICE

Family Muridae

Wood or long-tailed field mouse
Apodemus sylvaticus

VERDICT

Wood mice are the most common garden species, with a taste for seeds, nuts and fruit, but will also eat snails, worms, caterpillars and many insects. Mice will nest in sheds and outbuildings.

FOR THE DEFENCE

As long as crops and seeds are well protected, wood mice will do little damage and they will relish weed seeds. They can help to reduce the garden population of snails and unwelcome insects, and are carrion eaters. Many fall prey to owls, foxes and, invariably, domestic cats.

FOR THE PROSECUTION

Leave a row of newly planted pea seeds unprotected and you can be sure that the mice will find and eat them. As well as ripe fruit they can also dig up and nibble freshly set bulbs and corms. Adept jumpers, they will nibble boldly at the contents of bird feeders. Wood mice can dig into beds and borders to create hoards of food for the winter months.

THE TREATMENT

Cover newly planted seeds and bulbs with fine netting or fleece and peg it down very well to prevent agile mice from creeping underneath. Or try a deterrent of prickly gorse or holly sprigs. To protect young shoots, try growing them through large top and bottomless plastic bottles pushed into the soil. As a last resort, use humane mouse traps; poisoning in the garden is prohibited.

Know your wood mouse

- The typical wood mouse has a sandy-coloured coat, white underparts, large ears and a long tail.
- It will store fruit and nuts in abandoned birds' nests.
- The caps of fungi such as *Boletus* are a favourite food in autumn.
- In a single night, a mouse may travel as far as 400 m (¼ mile).
- Unlike house mice, wood mice have no unpleasant odour.
- Wood mice have acute senses and can easily detect the vibrations caused by the steps of an approaching wild animal, pet or human.
- The females give birth to as many as 6 litters a year, each comprising 4 to 8 young.
- A close relation, the yellow-necked mouse (*Apodemus flavicollis*) is also a British garden resident. As its name suggests it has a yellow band of fur around its throat. It is a little larger than the wood mouse.

Mouse lore

In folklore, mice are said to embody the soul, which may cause death by leaving a person's body during sleep. They are also believed to have been invented by witches, who conjure them from pieces of cloth.

MOLES

European mole *Talpa europaea*

Family Talpidae

VERDICT

Loathed by gardeners but loved by children, moles can make a total mess of your lawn or meadow with their molehills. These rarely seen mammals, most active in late winter and spring, devour useful earthworms, but also eat slugs, insect larvae, centipedes and millipedes.

FOR THE DEFENCE

There is much to admire in the work of these near-blind creatures with soft fur coats, and gardeners are best advised to live with them if they can. Moldy Warp, a character in Alison Uttley's *Little Grey Rabbit* books and Mole in Kenneth Graham's *Wind in the Willows* are endearing creatures.

FOR THE PROSECUTION

Excavating with their strong, spade-like forepaws, leaving mounds of fresh earth in their wake, moles can dislodge young flower and vegetable plants at their roots. As they work, earthworms, which are eaten in quantity, fall quickly and easily into their tunnels. Molehills need removing before you mow, and getting rid of moles may require professional help.

THE TREATMENT

Deterrence is the preferable treatment for coping with moles. Humane live-capture mole traps are available, but are best laid by professionals. It is no longer legal to sell mole deterrent smokes to gardeners.

• Try one of the many electronic buzzing devices designed to keep moles at bay.

• Before laying a turf lawn, especially if your garden is prone to damp, lay netting on the ground.

• Plant the caper spurge *Euphorbia lathyris* as a deterrent, a plant deemed effective by many gardeners.

That's amazing!

~~~ A mole will eat half its body weight (about 50 g/1¾ oz) in worms and other invertebrates every day.

~~~ In just a minute a mole can move over twice its body weight of earth.

~~~ Moles line their tunnels with leaves and moss.

~~~ If they come to the surface at night, moles are prey to foxes and to barn and tawny owls.

~~~ There are no moles in Ireland.

~~~ A mole will build an extra large molehill – a fortress – over its nesting chamber in early spring. Three or four young are born each summer.

~~~ In times past, every village had a mole catcher skilled in ridding farmers of moles which were also known as moldywarps.

RABBITS

European rabbit *Oryctolagus cuniculus*

Family Leporidae

VERDICT

Bold, hungry and prolific, rabbits may look pretty but can devastate an unprotected garden in no time. Even trees are not safe from their predations.

FOR THE DEFENCE

Rabbits are endearing characters in literature and have a long history in Britain as providers of meat and fur.

FOR THE PROSECUTION

Between dusk and dawn, but sometimes during daylight hours, rabbits will munch at your flowers, fruit and vegetables. They have a particular liking for new, soft growth, and in winter will even gnaw the bark from the bases of trees and shrubs, causing enough damage to be fatal to young specimens. Expert burrowers, they can dig holes and scrapes in lawns, beds and borders and worm their way under any less than perfect fencing. And rabbits can leap over low fencing!

THE TREATMENT

Keeping rabbits away from plants is the key to their control:
• Netting: use wire netting sunk into the ground around individual plants or small groups.
• Fencing: ideally use 25 mm (1 in) wire. Sink the bottom 30 cm (1 ft) into the ground and bend it outwards to prevent tunnelling, leaving 60–100 cm (2–3 ft) above ground.
• Tree guards: choose biodegradable spirals or wire netting.
• Repellents: sprays containing aluminium ammonium sulphate are available but not guaranteed effective. Never use them near edible plants.
• Plant choice: rabbits won't usually eat dahlias, hellebores, sunflowers or buddleia.

A furry history

 It was long thought that rabbits were brought to Britain by the Normans, but new findings date them to the Roman period.

 From Norman times they were nurtured in pillow mounds for their meat and fur. They were an important food for families during World War II.

 Britain's rabbit population, decimated in the 1950s by myxomatosis, currently numbers around 50 million.

 Rabbits hold an affectionate place in our literature, from Beatrix Potter's *The Tale of Peter Rabbit* to Richard Adams' *Watership Down*.

Lore and legend

• The original Easter bunny – a symbol of fertility – was not a rabbit but a hare.
• For fear of ill luck, the creature's name is never mentioned on Portland Bill in Dorset.

• To ensure good fortune, say 'rabbits' three times before going to sleep on the last day of each month – and 'hares' three times when you wake.
• Carrying a rabbit's foot for health and luck dates back to Roman times.

RATS

Brown rat *Rattus norvegicus*

Family Muridae

VERDICT

Fecund, disease-carrying invasive pests active all year. Making their homes in the garden, they will devour fruit, vegetables and pet and bird food (including chicken feed).

FOR THE PROSECUTION

From shelters under decking, greenhouses, garden sheds, compost bins and heaps and thick vegetation, rats venture out – usually at night – to feed on your apples and other fruit, and vegetables such as squashes, courgettes, parsnips, carrots and beetroot. They will also consume the nuts and seeds set out for birds, and any food remains not confined to the dustbin. Most seriously they can spread the bacterial disease leptospirosis (Weil's disease), a form of jaundice. The microbes excreted in rat urine enter human bodies through cut or grazed skin or by mouth.

FOR THE DEFENCE

Although loathed by the majority, 'domesticated', specifically bred rats can make good pets for those who like them. They are intelligent, and have acute senses.

Be a detective

You may see or hear rats on the move, but be aware of the evidence that rats will leave:

- Parallel grooves in vegetables and fruit made by the creatures' incisors.
- Tunnels in the soil with entrances measuring around 30 or 40 mm (1 or 1½ in) and 'rat runs' around the garden.
- Cylindrical faecal pellets about 15 mm (½ in) long, with rounded ends.

THE TREATMENT

If you discover one or more rats in the garden you can use traps or poison bait to kill them, but only formulations specifically approved for outdoor use. Always wear rubber gloves and dispose of any bodies by putting them in plastic bags in the dustbin. Alternatively, report the problem to your local authority which can arrange for professional v control. For safety, never put compost from a rat-infested bin or heap onto your fruit and vegetables.

Deterrence is the best way of avoiding rat problems.
• Block off access to spaces beneath sheds, decking and compost bins, and seal up any holes in garden buildings such as sheds.
• Be tidy. Remove rubbish, clear weedy areas and all food scraps from outdoor meals. Don't let excess food build up on bird tables; use squirrel-proof feeders.
• Deprive rats of the water essential to their lives. Fix any dripping outdoor taps and, in extreme cases, consider filling in a pond.
• Move pots and furniture around frequently – rats are discouraged by change.
• Get a dog.

SHREWS

Common shrew *Sorex araneus*

Family Soricidae

Ever-hungry shrews eat many garden pests but also beneficial worms and insects. They can inflict nasty bites if picked up.

FOR THE DEFENCE

In their constant battle to find enough food (they have to eat 80 to 90 per cent of their body weight daily in order to survive) shrews devour many unwanted garden creatures, notably slugs and snails, but also insect larvae and pupae of all kinds. They also eat mice. As prey for larger birds, including owls, they will attract these superb avians into the garden.

FOR THE PROSECUTION

Shrews eat valuable earthworms, spiders and beetles in large quantities. Domestic cats will pursue and kill them and they can attract foxes, magpies and jackdaws that are unwelcome to many gardeners. Shrews are territorial and aggressive. A bite from a shrew can be painful and cause a rash that may need medical attention.

THE TREATMENT

On the plus side ...
• **Encourage shrews by leaving gaps beneath sheds and hedges where they can hide and hibernate and rough grassy areas ideal for nesting.**
... and the minus
• **If you dislike shrews, catch them humanely in traps and release them in the countryside.**
• **Deter shrews by raking up leaves and foliage and cutting down tall grass.**

Did you know?

❀ There are an estimated 40 million shrews in Britain – the country's most common mammal – but they rarely live for more than two years.

❀ Only the tiny pigmy shrew (*Sorex minutus*) is found in Ireland.

❀ When attacked, shrews produce an evil-tasting secretion from glands in their skin, but this is a far from adequate protection from attack by cats or foxes which kill or injure them before this deterrent can take effect.

❀ 'Shrew' is an old term for a disagreeable woman, as in Shakespeare's *The Taming of the Shrew*, when the creature was known as a shrewmouse. Its name has no connection to cleverness described as 'shrewdness'.

❀ It was once deemed bad luck to see a shrew at the start of a journey.

❀ In English villages, 'shrew-ashes' were trees long believed to have healing powers supplied by a shrew whose dead body was incarcerated within them.

TOADS

Common toad *Bufo bufo*

Family Bufonidae

VERDICT

With prodigious appetites for slugs and other pests, toads — despite their looks — are excellent garden residents and are becoming ever rarer. They need water for breeding and shelter for hibernation.

FOR THE DEFENCE

As well as slugs, toads will devour caterpillars, beetles, woodlice, millipedes, spiders, ants and even small mice. They will attract hedgehogs into the garden because, unlike other predators, they are undeterred by the foul-tasting, toxic milky liquid toads secrete from their skin when threatened.

FOR THE PROSECUTION

Some people find the sight of toads repulsive, even to the point of phobia, particularly when, in spring, they migrate en masse from their winter quarters such as compost heaps to their breeding ponds. Some dubious garden visitors will feed on toads, including rats, crows and magpies.

THE TREATMENT

Encourage toads into the garden by providing a pond at least 60 cm (2 ft) deep with sloping sides for breeding and tadpole development. Piles of stones or wood near the pond margin will provide winter shelter, as will compost heaps, wood piles and the like. If you have toad homing routes into and through your garden, make sure you keep them clear.

Did you know?

- Toads 'home', returning to the same breeding pond every year by the same routes.
- A female may arrive for breeding already carrying a male on her back. But single females can be drowned by the attention of many males that form a 'toad ball' in the water.
- Of the 1,000 to 4,000 eggs laid by a female, only about 5 per cent will survive. The rest are eaten by fish, aquatic insects, dragonflies and newts.
- Toads have long been associated with witches as their 'familiars' or as witches in disguise.
- Toad skins were once used to get rid of warts and other skin complaints.
- An old cure for whooping cough and other illnesses was to hang a bag containing a toad (or parts of its body) around a person's neck.
- There are no toads in Ireland.

Toad or frog?

Tell a toad from a frog by looking for these characteristics:
- A warty, not a smooth skin.
- Crawling movements, not short, jumping ones made on shorter legs.
- Eggs laid in long strings, not clumps.
- No dark patch behind the eye.

VOLES

Field or short-tailed vole *Microtus agrestis*

Family Cricetidae

VERDICT

Small and largely vegetarian, these nocturnal rodents consume garden plants, particularly in autumn, and can damage tree bark. Voles are caught and eaten by owls, foxes, pet cats and other predators.

FOR THE DEFENCE

Voles are an essential part of the garden – and countryside – ecosystem. They are a vital food for owls, buzzards, kestrels and other birds of prey. Although mainly vegetarian, voles will also dine on insects and other invertebrate pests.

FOR THE PROSECUTION

Autumn plantings are particularly vulnerable to vole attack, whether bulbs, corms and tubers, or overwintering broad beans. They will also gorge on late summer crops such as sweetcorn, and munch through winter stores of potatoes, beetroot and carrots. Voles can strip brassica leaves down to their midribs, while they regard beech tree bark as a delicacy.

THE TREATMENT

Discourage voles by clearing up rough patches of grass where they like to build their nests and removing pieces of old wood under which they hide. Avoid using pesticides and herbicides that can poison and kill them. Protect vulnerable crops with netting or fleece and keep a check on those in storage.

Did you know?

- Voles are highly territorial and belligerent. Even in daylight hours you can hear the angry squeaks and chatterings of opposing adults.

- Between March and December voles rear 4 or 5 litters of 4 to 6 young which reach maturity at a mere 6 weeks.

- There are no field voles in Ireland, while on Orkney and Guernsey their place is taken by a subspecies of *Microtus arvalis*, the European common vole.

- Common names for the vole include dog mouse, grass mouse and ranny.

- 'Ratty' in Kenneth Grahame's *The Wind in the Willows* is a water vole (*Arvicola terrestris*), which you may be lucky enough to play host to if you have a large pond or stream running through the garden.

Vole dynamics

About every three to five years, vole populations increase extremely rapidly, producing a 'plague' of thousands. This is then followed by an equally speedy decline. Animals die from lack of food, but also from a surge in predator activity, especially that of barn and tawny owls. During times of plenty, cats will catch many voles in the garden and even bring them indoors as offerings to their owners after playing with them like toys.

Birds

While it is a joy to have birds in your garden, it is also fair to say that some are less welcome than others. Birds of all shapes and sizes can be guilty of enjoying your soft fruit, pecking at seedlings, or digging holes in your lawn. There are large bullies that scare off smaller species at the bird feeder and some will even steal the eggs of their avian relatives. On the plus side, birds are a vital part of the garden ecosystem, where their appetite for caterpillars and invertebrates of all kinds makes them invaluable. The garden bird population includes many more visitors than those included for detailed treatment here, such as robins, tits, finches, warblers and woodpeckers.

In the garden, the key to a good relationship with birds depends on the way your plot is equipped, maintained and managed. Bird feeders, in particular need careful thought. Design is critical, because most of the simplest feeders – and fat balls hung on branches – not only give instant access to big birds such as starlings, but will also encourage visits from grey squirrels and the like. And not all birds like to feed on the wing. A bird table, or food placed on the ground will be necessary for some, but again you need to be careful, especially if you have badgers nearby. For them, peanuts are an irresistible magnet.

To protect plants from hungry birds, netting is invaluable, but needs to be fine enough to prevent small birds from getting through it, or becoming trapped. It always needs to be pegged down well to stop them sneaking through at ground level. Fleece works perfectly for smaller plants. Deterrents of all kinds, which began centuries ago with the first scarecrows, can range from hanging up shiny objects like CDs to ultrasonic scarers, but the truth is that the birds are clever, especially the corvids, and will quickly become so adapted to their presence that they ignore them.

Nesting boxes can work well, but a more versatile way of encouraging birds to become garden residents is to provide plenty of cover in the form of climbers and hedging plants. Edible berries are also a draw, and are included in the plant lists at the end of the book. All birds are protected by law but, for their sake, give careful consideration to keeping cats out of your garden.

BLACKBIRDS

Common blackbird *Turdus merula*

Family Turdidae

VERDICT

Wonderfully vocal birds, with diets ranging from soft fruit to earthworms. Blackbirds will aggressively defend their nests before their fledglings depart. Their eggs are frequently taken by other garden visitors.

FOR THE DEFENCE

The fluid early morning songs of blackbirds are highlights of the dawn chorus and their notes add cheer to winter evenings. These beautiful birds have little fear of living close to humans and are remarkably fertile; if well fed they can raise five or six broods in one season. Snails feature in their wide, omnivorous diet. The pale turquoise eggs are vulnerable to attack by magpies and other birds, while fledglings can be taken by owls.

FOR THE PROSECUTION

Blackbirds are ardent fruit lovers, easily able to devastate currant and other berry crops, and they will also eat valuable earthworms, froglets and bees. Domestic cats are vulnerable to blackbird attacks, especially at critical times in the birds' lifecycle. They can become obsessed with mirrors placed in the garden or on cars, and will peck at them incessantly.

THE TREATMENT

• Protect fruit crops with netting fine enough to prevent birds from entering and peg it down well to stop them strolling in underneath it.
• Blackbirds are too heavy to use hanging feeders, so supply food on a bird table or the ground. They will thrive on mealworms and oats, and the fruit of ornamental shrubs (in which they may nest) such as elderflower, pyracantha and cotoneaster.
• Leave climbers such as honeysuckle unpruned to provide nesting sites.

In verse, lore and legend

🐦 The blackbirds 'baked in a pie' in the nursery rhyme 'Sing a Song of Sixpence' were almost certainly kept alive under a pastry crust and released for show at Tudor feasts.

🐦 In Celtic mythology, blackbirds were believed to carry messages to and from the underworld.

🐦 In some parts of England a blackbird pecking on the window is a sign of impending doom.

A tuneful relative

Speckle-breasted song thrushes (*Turdus philomelos*), much rarer than the blackbird, are also welcome garden visitors and renowned for their singing voices. Even if you don't see them you will appreciate the remains of their 'anvils' – the stones against which they beat snails to break their shells and consume the tasty flesh within.

CROWS

Carrion crow *Corvus corone*

Family Corvidae

VERDICT

It is no accident that the scarecrow has been a feature of cultivated land for many centuries. Crows and their close relations will eat virtually anything in the garden.

FOR THE DEFENCE

Crows can help to rid the garden of unwanted rats, mice and voles, and will peck at leatherjackets, slugs, snails, chafer grubs and other invertebrate pests. They are admirable for their intelligence and adaptability and can even be tamed.

FOR THE PROSECUTION

Whether singly or in flocks, raucous crows will almost indiscriminately eat your fruit and vegetables, take useful earthworms, frogs and toads, peck at your lawn and scare smaller birds away from bird feeders. They have even been known to take fish from garden ponds, rob the nests of other birds such as blackbirds for eggs and young, and even divebomb cats or other small pets. Many people think that they are unlucky.

THE TREATMENT

- **Netting over plants large and small is the best way of keeping crows from eating your crops. Make sure it is pinned down well to prevent birds from creeping underneath.**
- **Make a scarecrow, hang up old CDs, or fly 'flags' of polythene strips but be prepared for birds to adapt quickly to their presence and ignore them.**
- **Keep the garden free of food waste.**

It's a crow's life

○ Crows usually mate for life and rarely move far from their birthplace.

○ They are social creatures, with older siblings helping to raise younger chicks.

○ In proportion, crows have bigger brains than humans.

Crows 'speak' a variety of dialects in different parts of the country.

○ When predators such as hawks threaten them, crows will form mobs and attack viciously.

○ Left unharmed, a crow will live for about 15 years.

In myth and legend

- To the Chinese the crow embodies the spirit of the sun.
- In Australian aborigine legend the crow is black because its feathers were burnt in a fire set alight in retribution by the eaglehawk after the crow failed in its promise to babysit the eaglehawk's young.

- Seeing a single crow in flight was believed to foretell misfortune. If one was seen landing on the house, this presaged death.
- A crow is an insulting term for a bad-tempered old woman.

G

GULLS

Herring gull *Larus argentatus*

Family Laridae

Loud, messy scavengers resident all over Britain, gulls can cause serious damage if they nest on roofs, and can even attack pets. They are hard to deter, but admirably intelligent.

FOR THE DEFENCE

As more and more gull-edible material is being composted or burnt, gulls are becoming deprived of food and declining in numbers. Observing these intelligent and highly adaptable birds can be fascinating – as when they 'charm' earthworms to a lawn surface by stamping on the grass to simulate rainfall.

Leave any edible waste in your garden – even in flimsy or unsealed plastic bags – and you're liable to be invaded by gulls. They will defecate anywhere and everywhere and, if they nest on your roof, can block gutters and vents. Herring and black-backed gulls will dive bomb and snatch food from garden picnickers, and abductions of small dogs by gulls are reliably documented. More mundanely, they will take useful worms from your lawn. If encouraged, they can peck at and damage your hands.

THE TREATMENT

Prevention is the best way to deter gulls:
- **Use spikes, nets and wires to prevent access and nesting.**
- **Don't tempt gulls with food waste.**
- **Put red balloons in the garden or install wooden models of owls or hawks.**
- **Install windmill-like spinning propellers.**

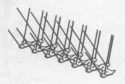

However
- **Remember that it is illegal to kill seagulls or destroy their nests yourself. In extreme circumstances you can ask your local authority for help as a last resort.**

In lore and legend

- It was once thought that seeing gulls inland was a sign of bad weather at sea. This may still be true to an extent, but there is no county in Britain that is now without gulls.

- According to legend, the infant St Cenydd was rescued from drowning off the Gower Peninsula around CE 550 and kept safe and warm with feathers the birds plucked from their own plumage.

- At the coast, gulls have learnt to pick up shells then drop them from a height to smash them and release their edible inhabitants.

HERONS

Grey heron *Ardea cinerea*

Family Ardeidae

VERDICT

Disliked by gardeners with well stocked ponds for their patient, efficient fishing abilities but otherwise herons are admirable large birds.

FOR THE DEFENCE

Herons are a delight to see in the garden, most likely standing stock still by a pond at dawn and dusk, and will eat slugs and snails from around its margins. Now protected by law, their numbers continue to increase, particularly in urban settings.

FOR THE PROSECUTION

Even young herons that have recently left the nest will come to fish in a garden pond. As well as devouring large quantities of fish, herons of all ages will swallow frogs, toads and small mammals such as shrews, plus dragonflies and damselflies.

THE TREATMENT

There are many ways to deter herons, although trial and error will undoubtedly pay dividends.

• Create vertical sides for a pond and place it near the house where herons are least likely to approach. Gentle slopes are herons' preference.

• Enclose the pond with shrubs – herons prefer more open settings.

• Put net over the pond – this is effective but unattractive.

• Plant plenty of vegetation in the pond such as water lilies to provide good hiding places for fish.

• Install a fountain to deter herons with ripples. Turn it on at dawn and dusk.

• Try a motion-activated cat-deterring sprinkler that will send out a jet of water if trodden on. Herons will stay away when it goes off.

• Place a plastic or ceramic imitation heron at the pondside – but be prepared for it to act as a heron lure!

Heron ways

- Herons nest in colonies or heronries, preferring tall trees to construct their platforms of sticks. The largest comprise more than 150 pairs of birds.

- They can forage for food up to 19 km (12 miles) from their nesting sites.

- Although now protected, herons once featured as food in ceremonial banquets (along with swans) up to the early 19th century.

- Other names for the heron include hernser, old Frank, Norry-the-bogs, Julie-the-bogs and hegri.

- If you see a heron, wish it 'good morning' to ensure the best of luck, especially if you're out on a fishing expedition alone.

- The Bennu bird of ancient Egypt, whose call was believed to have broken the silence of the original, uninhabited world, was depicted as a heron. It was a symbol of fertility and resurrection.

JACKDAWS

European jackdaw *Corvus monedula*

Family Corvidae

Noisy bullies at bird feeders, jackdaws will eat other birds' eggs. These highly intelligent birds eat fruit and valuable earthworms, but consume a wide range of unwelcome garden insects.

FOR THE DEFENCE

Jackdaws feed on caterpillars and a large range of insects as well as spiders and even mice. They will also eat the seeds of many common weeds. For those so inclined, jackdaws can be tamed to a certain degree.

FOR THE PROSECUTION

Once they discover that your garden is a good source of food, whether seed in feeders or ripe fruit such as strawberries or raspberries, jackdaws will return again and again, often en masse. They will tear up a lawn in the search for chafer bugs, and the eggs of robins, blackbirds and other birds are prey to jackdaw attention.

THE TREATMENT

- **Hang the feed for smaller birds in tubes that jackdaws find hard to deal with.**
- **Enclose fat balls in protective containers impenetrable to jackdaws.**
- **Provide food on the ground to discourage them from exploiting other sources.**
- **Protect ripe fruit with netting.**
- **Try using bird scarers, but be ready for the birds to ignore or adapt quickly to their presence.**
- **Make sure no scraps of food are left scattered in the garden – they will attract scavenging jackdaws.**

Did you know?

- Jackdaws are the smallest members of the crow family, distinguished by their ash-grey 'hoods' and calls that sound almost like yapping dogs.
- Britain has more than 1.4 million pairs of breeding jackdaws, with signs that numbers are continuing to increase.
- Chimneys are favourite nesting places for jackdaws.
- Seeing a jackdaw on the roof was once said to herald the arrival of a baby in the family – or could presage a death.

A holy bird

Like other corvids, jackdaws have a liking for shiny objects, a trait that led to a canonization. This is the story. Before he dined at a banquet the Archbishop of Rheims set his turquoise ring beside him as his hands were washed but the ring was stolen.

The cleric promptly cursed the human thief, not knowing that it was the bird but later, when the starving, limping jackdaw led the archbishop to the ring in its nest, it was pardoned and, eventually, made a saint.

MAGPIES

Magpie *Pica pica*

Family Corvidae

VERDICT

Bold, often disliked, black and white birds, magpies feed on insects and carrion but also on other birds' eggs and chicks. Subjects of many superstitions, they are increasing in numbers.

FOR THE DEFENCE

These intelligent birds, that collect shiny objects, will help to rid the garden of caterpillars, flies and leatherjackets, and may even eat small mice. They will enjoy eating kitchen scraps such as bacon rinds, particularly in winter.

FOR THE PROSECUTION

Magpies are certainly guilty of raiding the nests of tits, blackbirds, thrushes and robins, among others. They will devour unprotected soft fruits, eat earthworms and spiders, and bully small birds away from feeders and bird tables. When nesting, they can become particularly aggressive.

THE TREATMENT

Keep vulnerable fruit and vegetable plants well protected. Magpies can be scared away by hanging up shiny objects such as old CDs. Or, every so often, try playing recordings of rooks or crows cawing in distress. The Larsen trap for catching magpies totally unharmed, is legal as long as welfare regulations are strictly adhered to, but it is illegal to poison them. (See Wildlife and the law.)

A mixed reputation

The magpie's colouring is believed to be the result of its refusal to enter full mourning following the Crucifixion.

Whether good luck or bad is said to depend on the number of magpies seen together, according to the old rhyme, which has many versions.

One for sorrow, two for joy,
Three for a girl, four for a boy,
Five for silver, six for gold,
Seven for a secret, never to be told,
Eight for a wish, nine for a kiss
Ten for a bird, you must not miss.

If you see a single magpie there are many long established ways of dispelling any ill fortune, such as:

- Bow and say aloud 'Good morning to you Mr Magpie Sir'.
- Remove your hat.
- Spit over your right shoulder and say 'Devil, Devil I defy thee'.
- Keep an onion in your pocket all day.

The thieving habits of the magpie were the inspiration for Rossini's opera *La gazza ladra* of 1817.

Amazing behaviour

Magpies have been observed to hold vigils for dead birds, even collecting and laying grass at the site. They will also approach and gently peck at a corpse in a seemingly respectful gesture.

PHEASANTS

Family Phasianidae

VERDICT

Handsome game birds that can ravage country gardens. Bold, intelligent and bullies to smaller birds, they are not easily scared. Killing pheasants is legal within the shooting season.

Common (male) pheasant *Phasianus colchicus*

FOR THE DEFENCE

Superbly marked long-tailed birds, pheasants will help to rid the garden of unwanted wireworms, caterpillars and leatherjackets in summer. They will also eat voles and mice and remove moss from a lawn. Any pheasant eggs laid in the garden by the less colourful female are edible if fresh. For meat eaters, pheasant is a culinary delicacy.

In the Buddhist tradition pheasants are revered and protected, since killing them is regarded as a sin that will bring ill fortune.

FOR THE PROSECUTION

Because pheasants love to dig, potato and other root crops are particularly vulnerable to attack in late summer. The birds also have a predilection for fruit, flowers, seeds and leaves, peas and beans – almost anything in your garden, especially when 'wild' food is more scarce. Under the bird table, they will bully away small ground-feeding birds. Cats are wisely wary of pheasants, which can attack them and cause serious injuries.

THE TREATMENT

- **Keep crops covered. Use fleece or fine mesh netting.**
- **Try deterrents such as plastic birds of prey, spinners, old CDs and scarecrows.**
- **Set out a series of short sticks over a vegetable patch to deter birds – especially from taking dust baths.**
- **Provide food such as oats in the garden, but well away from vulnerable plants.**
- **Have a dog and let is spend plenty of time on your patch.**
- **Talk to your local gamekeeper and ask for a pheasant feeding hopper to be placed near (but not in) your garden.**

Birds of tradition

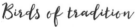

Natives of Asia, pheasants reached Britain in Roman times, but were well known as a delicacy to the ancient Greeks who discovered them in Colchis (present day Georgia), near the Black Sea – hence their specific name. Only in the Victorian era did artificial breeding begin to boost bird numbers for organized shoots.

The pheasants that visit your garden are unlikely to be truly wild. Rather they will be some of the 20 million and more birds (or their direct descendants) raised and released for sport in the UK every year.

The legal pheasant shooting season – for which you need a licence – is between October 1st and February 1st.

PIGEONS

Family Columbidae

Wood pigeon *Columba palumbus*

VERDICT

Easily able to decimate vegetable crops, pigeons will feast on soft fruit bushes and anything on a bird table, but are protected from being freely killed. Can possess remarkable homing abilities.

FOR THE DEFENCE

Agile birds with soft voices. 'Ordinary' pigeons or rock doves (*Columba livia*) are renowned for being able to fly huge distances and, in wartime, carry vital life-saving messages. They can form firm bonds with humans. Pigeons are close relatives of the doves long admired and kept in dovecotes in gardens.

Plants most vulnerable to pigeon attacks are cabbages and other brassicas, particularly when young. Leaves are often shredded down to their stalks. Other favourite foods are currants (buds and leaves as well as fruit) and cherries. Lilac leaves can also be pecked at. They will nest in garden trees and hedges and pigeon faeces can damage home and garden brickwork. Urban pigeons will eat bacon and other animal derived food scraps.

THE TREATMENT

Netting is the best protection against pigeons – a fine mesh will prevent them getting trapped. Make sure it is well pegged down at the base so that birds cannot get in underneath. By all means try other bird scaring devices to see what works for you.

Did you know?

- Pigeons can produce up to six broods of chicks in a single year.
- There are more than 3 million wood pigeons in Britain.
- Birds can dig up and eat small plants of turnips, carrots and other root crops.
- It's said that if you see a pigeon washing, rain is on the way.
- Homing pigeons were employed by the ancient Egyptians.

Garden residents

Rock doves have been kept in British gardens since the Norman Conquest of 1066, initially for their eggs, meat and feathers. Keeping doves was originally a privilege of the aristocracy, whose large, ornate dovecotes could house as many as 1,000 birds, leaving the crops of unhappy tenant farmers vulnerable to attack.

SPARROWS

Family Passeridae

House sparrow *Passer domesticus*

VERDICT

Welcome garden residents that will eat just about anything. Sparrows need suitable garden habitats to help prevent their numbers from declining further.

FOR THE DEFENCE

Sparrows add all kinds of insect pests to their highly varied diet, including aphids, feeding these to their young. They will relish the seeds of sunflowers planted for their enjoyment. As their name suggests, sparrowhawks will catch and eat them.

FOR THE PROSECUTION

Ripe fruits such as raspberries and strawberries are among the garden produce particularly favoured by sparrows. For no apparent reason, they peck at and decimate the petals of yellow spring flowers, especially crocuses. Flower and leaf buds can also be targeted.

THE TREATMENT

For the gardener …
Protect fruit from sparrow damage with fine netting and be sure to peg
it down well – sparrows are adept at squeezing through remarkably small
spaces. When planting crocuses, choose white and purple varieties to
prevent sparrow damage.

For the birds …
The recent decline in house sparrow numbers is a mystery, but avoid
using pesticides as far as possible. Not only do they destroy the insects
whose larvae are essential for chick rearing but appear to kill the birds by
remaining as a residue on seeds and other food. Because sparrows live in
family groups they need plenty of cover for nesting – shrubs grown close
together are ideal.

That's amazing!

- The association between sparrows and humans goes back at least 10,000 years.
- The sparrow was sacred to the love goddesses Aphrodite and Venus.
- Because of their abundance and obvious sexual behaviour sparrows were once synonymous with vulgarity, lewdness and anything uncouth.
- In the early 1900s sparrows were regarded as pests. Members of Sparrow Clubs destroyed millions of birds and their eggs.
- Sparrows will aggressively defend their nesting sites.
- Research carried out in the 1940s detected 838 different types of food in sparrows' stomachs.

No relation

The hedge sparrow or dunnock (*Prunella modularis*) may share the house
sparrow's name but belongs to a totally different zoological family. It is easy to
distinguish, having a slender beak, used for eating a wide variety of insects, and a
distinctive totally grey head.

S

STARLINGS

Common starling *Sturnus vulgaris*

Family Sturnidae

Noisy, tenacious birds, starlings descend on the garden in flocks. Disliked for their greedy habits and iridescent, 'oily-looking' plumage, but a species that is in serious decline.

FOR THE DEFENCE

Starlings help garden lawns by consuming large quantities of leatherjackets, cranefly larvae which can destroy grass from its roots, leaving bare patches. Flies, ants, spiders and millipedes are also favoured foods. These birds are remarkable mimics and a group of starlings, known as a murmuration, is a magnificent sight, especially in winter.

FOR THE PROSECUTION

As they peck for insects, starlings can make holes in lawn turf. Bullies at the garden feeder, they will scare or fight off smaller birds. A starling flock can strip fruit bushes and trees of their bounty with amazing speed. And if they roost in quantity on the roofs of your house, their droppings can erode and damage the stonework. They can even fall down unprotected chimneys into the fireplace.

THE TREATMENT

Keep starlings under control by selecting some bird feeders designed to be accessible only to smaller birds. Fruit bushes can be well protected with bird-proof netting but it is practically impossible to stop them from feasting on tree fruits such as cherries and apples.

Nature's linguists

Starlings are rightly admired for their ability to mimic a huge range of sounds, from owl hoots, frog croaks, and chickens' clucks to telephone rings and human voices. They can even wolf whistle.

The Roman naturalist Pliny the Elder claimed that he taught starlings to speak both Latin and Greek.

The birds were once favourite pets. The composer Mozart not only taught a bird to sing but is believed to have incorporated the tune into his Piano Concerto in G Major (K453). When the bird died he gave it an elaborate funeral at which he recited a poem he had written in memory of his 'little fool'.

Worth protecting

The squabbling, voracious behaviour of starlings is no more than the epitome of creatures that are naturally gregarious. Each individual feeds quickly, simply to survive competition from its neighbours. Surveys by the RSPB have recorded a decline of more than 65 per cent in bird numbers in Britain since the 1970s.

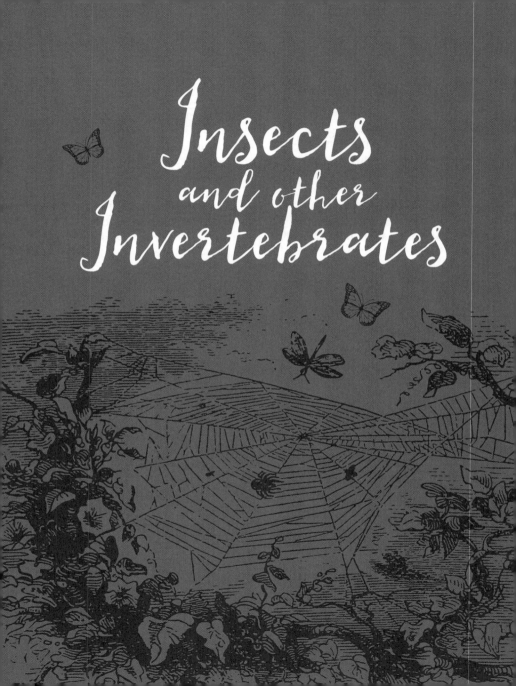

Insects
and other
Invertebrates

Of all the wildlife in your garden the majority of species – by far – are insects and other invertebrates. Inevitably your attitude towards them will depend, to a large extent, on the effect that they have on your plants for good or ill, but what is far more important is the place that each of them has in the garden ecosystem. So while there is no doubt that slugs can shred a bed of hostas overnight, the slugs themselves are a vital food for hedgehogs, frogs and birds of all kinds. Birds also depend on caterpillars and a huge range of other larvae, as well as mature insects, for their continued well-being. Perhaps most essentially of all, the invertebrate population of the garden plays a vital role in pollination, both within the confines of your plot and far beyond.

The challenge for every gardener is to maintain a balance between damage and benefit, of which there is no better example than the relationship between ladybirds and aphids. Ladybird larvae, which look like miniature crocodiles, have a voracious appetite for scale insects and particularly for aphids – blackfly, whitefly, and the like – but if you use a pesticide to kill the aphids you will almost certainly destroy the ladybirds at the same time. Earwigs may well damage your prize dahlias but they, too, are brilliant aphid eaters.

As the subjects of this chapter reveal, many insects and invertebrates have evolved to depend largely for food on one particular type of plant and often at a particular time of year. Carrot flies, cabbage white caterpillars and asparagus and lily beetles are perfect examples. This makes it essential to understand their life cycles so that you can take appropriate action to avoid trouble, as far as possible, or to restrict chemical pest control to an absolute minimum.

The details of insect and invertebrate life included in this chapter, combined with the lists at the back of the book, will help you to work out which plants will best create a harmonious balance between predator and prey. At the same time, they will also help to attract the most useful species to the garden, whether they be pollinating honey and bumble bees, soil improving earthworms or woodlice and other creatures that help to decompose garden debris. Such practice, especially if you have water in the garden, will also bring you beautiful carnivorous dragon and damsel flies.

ANTS

Family Formicidae

Common black ant *Lasius niger*

VERDICT

Successful social insects, ants are a nuisance because they 'farm' aphids, protecting them from attack. Nest-building ants can disturb plant roots and leave mounds of earth on lawns.

FOR THE DEFENCE

It is hard not to admire the diligence and ingenuity of ants. They are a useful food for birds, which also catch and rub ants over their feathers. As they do so the ants release formic acid, which can help to kill mites, bacteria and fungi. Ants can help to control pests such as sawflies.

Ants have a special relationship with aphids annoying to gardeners, literally guarding them against being eaten by ladybirds, spiders and other natural pest controllers and, in return, receiving nutritious secretions of honeydew. They will even bite the wings off aphids to prevent them from flying away, or carry them to less crowded locations. A similar relationship can exist between ants and scale insects. Ant nests can be a bother, especially when constructed near plant roots. Red ants can deliver nasty stings.

THE TREATMENT

- **Whenever possible, leave ants alone. In extreme circumstances try watering in a nematode based biological control.**
- **Disperse anthills on a lawn with a stiff brush.**
- **Never use an ant remedy formulated for indoor use in the garden.**

The amazing colony

- Queen ants are fertile, winged females that swarm with males on the wing in late summer. After mating, the males die. The many worker ants are sterile, wingless females.

- Ants have incredible powers of communication. Using scent and touch they pass messages to each other about everything from the location of food supplies to the risk of imminent attack.

- Black ant colonies can be invaded and taken over by another species *Lasius umbratus* which kill the queen and enslave her workforce.

More garden ants of different kinds

Wood ants (*Formica rufa*) eat moth and sawfly caterpillars after killing them with formic acid injections.
Red ants (*Myrmica ruginodis*) nest under tree stumps or in loose bark.

They can inflict painful stings.
Jet black ants (*Lasius fuliginosus*) climb to great heights to feed on giant oak aphids. They nest in tree stumps.

APHIDS

Greenfly *Aphis* sp

Superfamily Aphidoidea

VERDICT

Various species of sap-sucking insects, including greenfly and blackfly, that weaken plants and encourage disease, but essential food for creatures that are key members of the garden ecosystem.

FOR THE DEFENCE

From ladybirds, lacewings and hoverflies to ants, earwigs, beetles, moths, butterflies and birds, all manner of garden wildlife depend on aphids for food. Many of these are vital pollinators and scavengers in the garden. Apart from the creatures themselves, their big attraction is the sticky, sugar-rich honeydew that aphids secrete. Robins and other small birds will eat aphids.

FOR THE PROSECUTION

Aphids clustering on roses and other plants don't look good. And as they infest plants from roses to apples, aphids can literally suck the life from them. As they suck sap they cause weakness and distortion, spread viruses and create conditions ideal for the growth of unsightly and damaging sooty moulds. Many aphids have links with specific plants (see below).

THE TREATMENT

Tolerate aphids as much as you can, otherwise watch out for them, especially in spring when plants are most vulnerable, and deal with them early.
For minor attacks, simply rub them off plant stems and leaves (wear gloves) or try hosing them off.
For broad beans, nip out the top cluster of leaves.
Use an insecticide as a last resort (see Pesticides and how to use them), but remember that even organic or home-made ones, such as garlic spray or soap solution, will kill ladybirds and other valuable invertebrates as well as the aphids.

That's amazing!

Aphids appear in swarms almost overnight because they reproduce themselves without sex. Inside each female or 'stem mother' dozens of identical offspring are produced and released within days. If not killed prematurely, hatched aphids live for 20 to 40 days.

The sticky mess that aphids leave behind them is honeydew. Aphids get their energy from the sugary sap of the plants they feed on, but because they consume more than they need the excess is secreted and, in turn, is the magnet for so many other creatures. Ants will even 'milk' the honeydew as it emerges in tiny bubbles from aphids' mouthparts.

Many aphids have evolved to become dependent on specific plants. Key examples include the woolly beech aphid, sycamore aphid, cabbage aphid, rose aphid and peach-potato aphid.

ASPARAGUS BEETLES

Crioceris asparagi

Family Chrysomelidae

VERDICT

The beetle infestation that every asparagus grower dreads. Controlling these pretty insects organically takes care and effort. The larvae link significantly into the garden food chain.

FOR THE DEFENCE

Asparagus beetles are undoubtedly attractive; equally their larvae are important food for beneficial lacewings and spiders. The beetles do not affect ornamental types of asparagus grown in the herbaceous border.

FOR THE PROSECUTION

Because asparagus takes so long to mature and establish itself in the garden, the sight of asparagus beetles on plants is depressing to any vegetable gardener. Both the dark grey, slug-like larvae and the black, yellow and red adult beetles eat the plants' leaves and stems, even gnawing through the bark, so weakening and distorting plants that may then turn brown. Such serious damage can affect the crop in subsequent years. Infestations from neighbouring gardens or allotments are virtually impossible to prevent.

THE TREATMENT

There is no insecticide safe to use in the garden to combat the asparagus beetle, but all these actions will help to deal with attacks:
• **Watch out for rows of eggs, then larvae, in April, or as soon as spears emerge above ground; squash and/or rub them off. Wear gloves. Be prepared for new 'crops' of larvae throughout the summer.**
• **Pick off the adults and drown them in water, being extra vigilant in May, just ahead of the harvest season.**
• **Crop young spears every couple of days up to the end of June.**
• **Cut down and destroy old fronds in autumn – burn them or take them to your recycling centre.**
• **Weed the asparagus bed very thoroughly all year and in autumn remove any fallen leaves to help remove sites in which adults can overwinter.**

Pretty pests

Many other attractive beetles belong to the same family as asparagus beetles, all of them known as leaf beetles. Apart from the lily and Colorado beetles (see Flea beetles) two others types the gardener may encounter are:

🖉 Mint beetles (*Chrysolina* spp): bright metallic green or blue insects that can chew off the leaves of affected plants almost overnight.

🖉 The rosemary leaf beetle (*Chrysolina americana*): an emigrant from America that will eat thyme, sage and lavender as well as its namesake. Its rounded green body is distinctively striped in red.

BOX CATERPILLARS

Family Crambidae

Box tree moth *Cydalima perspectalis*

VERDICT

The caterpillars of this immigrant moth can totally devastate box plants. If not removed, their attacks can prove fatal. Ranked as a top garden pest in Britain.

FOR THE DEFENCE

Blue tits have been known to eat the caterpillars but there is little else to say in their defence. Caterpillar damage is not to be confused with box tree blight, a fungal disease.

FOR THE PROSECUTION

Box tree caterpillars, unmistakably coloured yellow and green with black and white stripes, not only rapidly strip the leaves from plants but cover them with an unsightly webbing. The damage inflicted is often fatal and you may have to abandon box altogether as a garden ornamental.

THE TREATMENT

Vigilance is key to coping with these caterpillars.
• Look out for eggs on leaf undersides and rub them off by hand.
• Remove caterpillars by hand and kill them. Ditto pupae.
• Set up pheromone traps (see Biological controls). These will help you monitor when the moths are most active.
• Consider replacing box with other plants (see below).
• Try a nematode preparation suitable for fruit and vegetables, although success is likely to be patchy.
• Use a home-made soap-based insecticide which is least likely to damage other invertebrates.
• Spray with an organic pesticide containing natural pyrethrins or a non-organic systemic pesticide, following instructions. Never use these near plants in flower.
• For a severe infestation, seek professional advice.

Know your enemy

The box tree moth, native to East Asia, was first seen in Britain in 2007 and has since become established countrywide. London is particularly affected. Some tell-tale signs of box caterpillar attacks include:

Eggs are laid in overlapping sheets on leaf undersides.

Young caterpillars have black heads and green and yellow bodies. White bodies and stripes develop as they mature.

Caterpillars metamorphose into pupae held in whitish webbing.

Adults usually have white wings bordered in brown, but can be totally brown. The wingspan is about 4 cm (1½ in).

Some good alternatives

If your box dies off, it is best to replant with an alternative shrub. Some good replacements include small, compact varieties of berberis, euonymus, lavender, pittosporum, podocarpus, holly, rosemary, rhododendrons and yew.

BUMBLEBEES

Garden bumblebee *Bombus hortorum*

Family Apidae

VERDICT

Essential, attractive garden pollinators from early in the year, and food for robins and other birds, bumblebees should be well provided for. However, they can nest in inconvenient locations.

FOR THE DEFENCE

Bumblebees are particularly good pollinators because they can literally shake the tightly adhering pollen out of the flowers they visit. Because they are spurred into action when the temperature is as low as 10°C, queen bumblebees can even begin flying in January to start their important work of pollination, carried out as they begin nest building.

FOR THE PROSECUTION

House eaves, cavity walls, air bricks, compost heaps, spaces beneath patio paving and garden sheds are all ideal sites for bumblebee nests. These are made mainly from grass and moss, and can be a garden nuisance. Bumblebee stings are rare (and some species are even stingless).

THE TREATMENT

If you discover a bumblebee nest, leave it alone. Never attempt to move it – if practicable, try re-routing the nest entrance. Avoid breathing on the nest, which can aggravate the inmates. If you still have problems, contact the Bumblebee Conservation Trust.

To encourage bumblebees:
• Plant a wide variety of flowers to provide nectar and pollen from January onwards. (See Plants for wildlife). Unlike honeybees they 'browse' from species to species.
• Erect purpose-made bumblebee houses, or make them yourself.
• Don't tidy the garden too much. Bumblebees need leafy sites to hibernate in during winter and like to nest on sunny banks and under trees.
• If badgers visit your garden, protect any bumblebee nests with chicken wire.

That's extraordinary!

- Bumblebees are named for their hums – to bumble is to buzz. They are also called dumbledores and foggie-bummers.
- At low temperatures they have the unique ability to warm themselves up by using their body chemistry to 'rev up' their flight muscles.
- Unlike honeybees, bumblebees can sting twice before they die.
- Bumblebees have to eat almost continuously to stay alive.
- As they land on flowers the bees deposit an odorous, oily 'footprint' telling their associates that there is no nectar available there any longer.
- Worker bumblebees will fan a nest with their wings to cool it down.
- Britain has 24 species of bumblebees.

CABBAGE WHITE CATERPILLARS

Large white *Pieris brassicae*

Family Pieridae

VERDICT

Seriously damaging and hard to control larvae of two butterfly species, particularly affecting brassicas, but also other plants, including some weeds. The adult butterflies are valuable pollinators.

FOR THE DEFENCE

Sparrows and goldfinches are able to tolerate eating cabbage white caterpillars, as are spiders, which will also eat the adults. Small whites are good food for beetles, harvestmen and other members of the garden food chain and are eaten by parasitic wasps; the butterflies will lay their eggs on many weed species, especially those with white or blue flowers.

Butterfly lore

- ✿ It's said that if the first butterfly you see in spring is white then prosperity is assured for the coming months. This dates to a time when white bread was a luxury.

- ✿ Butterflies are believed to represent the souls of the departed. White butterflies are also said to be angels in insect form.

FOR THE PROSECUTION

Caterpillars of both the large and the small white (*P. rapae*) will strip to their ribs the leaves of cabbages, broccoli, Brussels sprouts, turnips and also nasturtiums and spoil leaves with their droppings. Because they accumulate mustard oil in their bodies as they feed, they are unpalatable to many birds.

THE TREATMENT

Prevent and treat brassica massacre this way:
• **Keep vulnerable plants covered with fine netting, well pegged down.**
• **Remove eggs and caterpillars by hand and squash or drown them.**
• **Try companion planting (see Good gardening practice) with marigolds or, in the vegetable garden, plant nasturtiums as a 'sacrificial' crop.**
• **Spray young caterpillars as they hatch with the nematode biological control *Steinernema carpocapsae*.**
• **Use an insecticide containing pyrethrum, making repeat applications every few days.**
• **As a last resort use a stronger insecticide containing synthetic pyrethroids, but follow the instructions to the letter (see Pesticides and how to use them).**

Know your enemy

Large white Adults have more prominent pairs of black spots on their upper wings and darker wing tips. Bristly green, black and yellow caterpillars hatch in groups.

Small white Wings are narrower and the lower ones yellower. Well camouflaged velvety green caterpillars hatch singly, almost always on leaf undersides.

CARROT FLIES

Carrot root fly *Psila rosae*

Order Diptera

VERDICT

The larvae of this small fly damage the roots of carrots and their close relations severely enough to make them inedible. The problem, impossible to solve with pesticides, demands extreme vigilance from the vegetable gardener.

FOR THE DEFENCE

The fly's efficiency continues to stimulate breeders to create resistant varieties and plant scientists to develop biological controls.

FOR THE PROSECUTION

As they feed, carrot fly larvae, which hatch from eggs laid in late May to June and again in August and September, create a network of tunnels. These show up as dark, rusty coloured scars only when the carrot crop is lifted, but above ground the leaves can turn yellow. Parsnips, celery and celeriac roots can also be affected. Sometimes, the slim creamy-yellow grubs can be seen crawling out.

THE TREATMENT

Prevention is the key to deterring carrot fly.

• Choose more resistant varieties such as 'Fly Away', 'Resistafly' and 'Styan'.

• The flies are attracted to carrot aromas generated by bruised foliage, so sow seed sparsely to avoid thinning. Mixing seed with fine sand can work.

• Wait to sow seeds until mid May, after the first generation of larvae have matured and before the second egg-laying phase in August.

• Mix carrots with companion plants (see below).

• Protect plants with fine netting, fleece or a polytunnel.

• Plant seeds in containers that can be placed high up. The flies never venture more than 60 cm (2 ft) from the soil surface.

• Water on a nematode biological control. In spring choose *Steinernema feltiae*, in summer *S. carpocapsae*.

• Mulch with grass cuttings to close off the soil crevices favoured for egg laying. This will also encourage ground beetles and centipedes that eat the larvae.

• Choose your windiest, most exposed site. Carrot flies are weak fliers preferring still air.

• To avoid population build up (flies can overwinter) rotate crops every year.

• Install sticky yellow traps on sticks placed near the soil surface.

Companion plants

Success is by no means assured, but it is worth trying to mix the carrot crop with plants that may deter carrot flies.

• Members of the allium family – the smell of onions, shallots, garlic and chives can be effective.

• Strong smelling herbs such as rosemary and sage.

• When sowing, mix carrot seeds with those of feathery-leaved annuals such as cosmos and French marigolds.

CODLING MOTHS

Codling moth *Cydia pomonella*

Family Tortricidae

VERDICT

Codling moth caterpillars severely damage crops of apples, pears and quinces, eating them from the inside. But beware: a caterpillar in an apple could be an apple sawfly larva.

FOR THE DEFENCE

Codling moth caterpillars are savoured by blue tits, great tits and treecreepers. They are also eaten by earwigs.

FOR THE PROSECUTION

Codling moths lay their eggs into the fading flowers of apples and other fruit, ensuring that when these hatch they have a ready supply of food. Until the internal damage is exposed in the ripe fruit, the only signs of entry are minute holes almost impossible to detect. The exit hole is larger and usually visible towards the 'eye' or top of the fruit.

THE TREATMENT

Useful strategies include:
• Tie strips of corrugated cardboard around tree trunks – the caterpillars will spin their cocoons here, rather than in the soil, and can be removed in the winter.
• Buy and hang up pheromone traps. These are 'baited' with pellets of the powerful, naturally produced scents which lure males to their mates. In the garden a trap can often attract enough males to inhibit mating significantly and reduce the number of eggs that are laid.
• Spray a nematode preparation on tree trunk and branches in autumn.
• As a last resort, use an insecticide, ideally in combination with a pheromone trap. Never spray when plants are in flower or you will kill all pollinators.

A moth's life

Once they have munched on fruit flesh and are fully grown, codling moth caterpillars emerge from the fruit. They crawl downwards, coming to rest in crevices in the tree bark where they overwinter, forming chrysalises. From these, adult males and females hatch in spring, then mate. Finally, the females lay their eggs, which look like minute dew drops, into the fading blossom where they hatch and resume the creature's life cycle.

What's in a name?

The codling moth is probably named from the codlin, an ancient variety of British apple, although in Saxon times cod-apple was the name for a quince. 'Wormy apples' have certainly been recorded since Roman times.

C

CUTWORMS

Turnip moth *Agrotis segetum*

Family Noctuidae

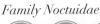

VERDICT

When cutworms (caterpillars of several nocturnal moth species) bite, they can damage plant parts enough to deal death blows. They are an important food for many welcome garden residents, and the adults are pollinators.

FOR THE DEFENCE

Cutworms are enjoyed by ground beetles, hedgehogs and many garden birds, especially warblers. The adult moths are good food for bats, birds and spiders.

FOR THE PROSECUTION

Most cutworms, usually coloured grey, pale green or cream, live in the soil from where they emerge on warm, dry summer and early autumn nights to feed on plant roots and stem bases as well as any accessible foliage. Leafy salads, brassicas and root crops are all vulnerable, as are sunflowers and clematis. A severe attack can literally cut down a young plant, causing sudden, extreme wilting. Cutworms will overwinter in the soil, survive all but extreme frosts and emerge in mild spells.

THE TREATMENT

Vigilance and organic treatments are the best ways to control cutworms, which typically curl into a tight 'c' shape when disturbed.
• Go out with a torch at night to locate, remove and kill the larvae.
• Keep weeds under control – they can harbour cutworms around their roots.
• Water well in dry weather; young cutworms will not survive if they become very wet.
• Protect plants with fleece or netting.
• Dig the soil well over the winter – cutworms that come to the surface will be ready bird food.
• Apply a nematode preparation, following the maker's instructions.
• Hang pheromone traps (see Biological controls) to monitor when the adult moths are most active (they can lay their eggs from May through to August).

All in the family

Apart from the turnip moth, among the other night flying moths commonly responsible for producing damaging cutworms are the yellow underwing (*Noctua pronuba*), the heart and dart moth (*Agrotis exclamationis*) and the cabbage moth (*Mamestra brassicae*).

Although they appear dull brown or grey when at rest with their wings folded flat, many of the moths in this family expose bright colours such as red, orange, yellow and blue when in flight. These are the aptly named underwings, whose hues are thought to be used to scare off predators.

EARTHWORMS

Family Lumbricidae

Common earthworm *Lumbricus terrestris*

VERDICT

Essential for healthy soil, but on lawns and gravel can leave unsightly casts. Invaluable food for hedgehogs, birds and many other garden residents. Some earthworms can be 'cultivated' for making liquid fertilizer.

FOR THE DEFENCE

As they pull dead vegetation from the surface and burrow down into soil, earthworms 'dig', aerate and enrich the soil, significantly increasing its fertility. The better your soil – or the compost in your heap – the more earthworms will flourish. Despite their looks, worm casts are rich in minerals.

FOR THE PROSECUTION

Some earthworms, but particularly those such as green worms (*Allolobophora chlorotica*) and their close relations create worm casts. These excreted muddy soil-filled coils are an ideal growing medium for moss and weeds.

THE TREATMENT

Use a wire rake to break up and disperse worm casts once they have dried out.

Earthworms fail to thrive in very acidic or dry soils, so correct these by adding lime and water as necessary. Don't waste energy removing leaf litter from the soil – leave it for the worms, and reduce digging to a minimum. And consider making a wormery.

Worm-made compost

A shed or sheltered garden site is ideal for a wormery, essentially a bin with two compartments, the upper one containing worms plus organic waste, the lower one a sump where liquid fertilizer accumulates. Some key tips for a good wormery include:

- Choose brandling, red or tiger worms, which can be bought from specialist suppliers.
- Keep the wormery moist but not waterlogged.
- Choose a frost-free site.
- Avoid adding fatty foods and tough, woody garden waste, but do add teabags coffee grounds and small amounts of shredded newspaper.

That's amazing!

- Earthworms can survive if cut in two with a garden spade.
- Charles Darwin studied earthworms intensively for over 40 years. He discovered that they are extremely sensitive to vibrations, which stimulate them to come to the surface.

- There are 25 species of earthworms native to Britain. The largest, the lobworms, will travel long distances across the soil surface to find mates.
- Mixtures containing dried earthworms were once used to treat everything from epilepsy to jaundice.

EARWIGS

Common earwig *Forficula auricularia*

Order Dermaptera

VERDICT

Earwigs will attack the petals of dahlias and other flowers, but also feed on aphids and other garden pests, including codling moths and their caterpillars which can severely damage apple crops.

FOR THE DEFENCE

As well as aphids, earwigs include mites, nematodes and decaying vegetable matter in their diet. Thriving in damp places, they are a favourite food of frogs, toads and newts.

FOR THE PROSECUTION

Feeding in the hours of darkness, earwigs will eat holes in, or munch deep into the petals of dahlias, clematis, chrysanthemums, zinnias, marigolds and other flowers. Young leaves of these plants, as well as vegetable seedlings, are also vulnerable to earwig damage as are soft fruits. If you pick up an earwig it may inflict a painful bite with its forceps-like pincers, but it does not produce any venom.

THE TREATMENT

Hunt out, deter or trap earwigs in a variety of ways:
- Go out into the garden at night with a torch and pick off any earwigs you see and dispose of them.
- Rub petroleum jelly on the stems of prize plants to stop earwigs in their tracks.
- Lay empty halves of oranges or grapefruit on the ground – earwigs will be tempted inside by the warmth, especially if the ground is damp.
- Make traps by stuffing upturned flowerpots with hay or straw and setting them on top of canes inserted into the ground near vulnerable plants.
- Never spray plants that are in flower, but control extensive earwig damage at other times with a spray such as deltamethrin as a last resort.

A memorable name

No one knows how earwigs got their name but they have a centuries old reputation of being able to crawl into the ears of sleeping humans. There is certainly a true story of a Cornishman driven mad by a weird sensation in his ear, caused indeed by an earwig.

The name could also come from the creature's wings which, although rarely unfolded, are ear shaped.

The French call them *perce-oreilles* (ear piercers), the Germans *Ohrwürmer* (ear worms). Of the many other common names these are among the most descriptive: arrywiggle, battle twig, coachman, forky-tail, narrow-wiggle, pincher-wig and twitch-bell.

EELWORMS

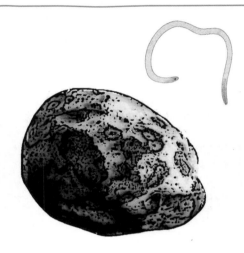

Potato damaged by potato eelworm
Globodera sp

Order Nematoda

VERDICT

Microscopic soil-dwelling nematode worms, eelworms severely damage or even kill vegetables and flowers by puncturing and feeding on plant cells. Prevention from attack is as yet the only cure.

FOR THE DEFENCE

Many benign eelworms live harmlessly in the soil, feeding on fungi and bacteria. Some are even bred specifically for inclusion in biological pest control preparations.

FOR THE PROSECUTION

Eelworms of different species will attack potatoes, tomatoes, onions, salad crops, soft fruits, bulbs and flowers such as phlox, penstemons, chrysanthemums and dahlias. Not only can their eggs survive for up to 10 years in the soil but they can act as vectors for serious viral diseases. It is important to be able to recognize the damage caused by different types of worm (see opposite).

Preventing egg build up in the soil and recognizing the symptoms of attack are key. Burn and destroy all affected plant material or take – and declare it – to your recycling centre. Keep your soil weed free.

Potato cyst eelworms – attack potatoes, tomatoes and aubergines

Symptoms: Leaves yellow, then blacken and the plant dies. Small potato tubers contain small lumps. (These cysts contain the egg-filled bodies of dead females.)
Prevention: Rotate crop positions annually, re-using each site as little as possible. Choose eelworm resistant varieties such as 'Pentland Javelin', 'Kestrel' and 'Maris Piper'. Grow tomatoes in growbags or freshly bought compost, never garden soil.

Stem and bud eelworms – attack bulbs and herbaceous perennials

Symptoms: bulbs develop distorted leaves and flowers or split and rot. When cut in half, brown rings can be seen. Stems of flowering plants (particularly phlox, hydrangeas and campanulas) swell and leaves fail to form beyond the midrib.
Prevention: Dig up bulbs and start with fresh stock. Rotate garden positions and vary plant choices. Search for resistant varieties.

Leaf and bud eelworms – attack herbaceous perennials

Symptoms: In late summer, lower leaves brown in angular patches; the problem then moves up the plant stem. Most susceptible are chrysanthemums, Japanese anemones, penstemons and dahlias.
Prevention: Water plants from the roots to help reduce the risk of spread. Rotate garden positions and vary plant choices. Look out for resistant varieties.

BEWARE!
Never, ever, put plants infested with eelworm on the compost heap – even their burnt remains.

FLEA BEETLES

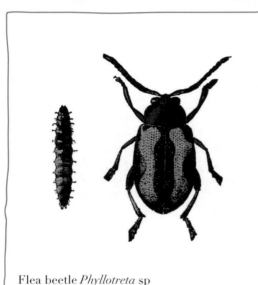

Flea beetle *Phyllotreta* sp

Family Chrysomelidae

VERDICT

Adept jumping beetles that chew holes in the leaves of brassicas and some other vegetables and salads. They can also attack wallflowers, alyssums and nasturtiums. The larvae can damage young plant roots.

FOR THE DEFENCE

Flea beetles can be useful garden pollinators and the larvae, particularly, good food for ladybirds.

FOR THE PROSECUTION

Small round 'shot holes' chewed into leaves, which later turn brown, are a sure sign of flea beetle attack, and you may well see these aptly named beetles jumping off plant leaves as you approach. The young plants of cabbages, sprouts, radishes, rocket and Chinese cabbage are particularly vulnerable to attack.

THE TREATMENT

• Don't plant or sow too early in the season – waiting will help to ensure stronger plants and coincide with a drop in the flea beetle population that reaches its height in early spring.

• Cover small plants with fleece or fine netting to prevent beetles from jumping onto vulnerable leaves.

• Prevent adult beetles from surviving their winter hibernation by clearing away leaves and other debris that are their favoured habitats.

• Dig the soil well in the autumn to help eradicate adult beetles, which can also overwinter in the soil.

• Plant 'trap' crops such as radishes – the beetles may attack the leaves but will leave the edible roots undamaged.

• Use a nematode worm preparation to kill the larvae.

• If you need to resort to an insecticide, choose an organic preparation such as neem oil, but never use it near plants that are in flower.

• Sprinkle on some diatomaceous earth, a powder that will deter the beetles by irritating their exoskeletons.

Meet the relatives

From their preferred food, flea beetles are classified as leaf beetles. Other members of the group include:

Lily beetles (*Lilioceris lilii*): bright red adults which, true to their name, munch and damage lilies.

Rainbow leaf beetles (*Chrysolina cerealis*): rare creatures unlikely to be seen in the garden or indeed elsewhere, and now afforded legal protection.

Colorado potato beetles (*Leptinotarsa decemlineata*): black and yellow striped introductions from North America that can decimate crops. If seen they must, by law, be reported to DEFRA.

GROUND BEETLES

Family Carabidae

VERDICT

These archetypal black beetles are vital to the garden ecosystem, feeding on many different invertebrates, particularly slugs and snails. They devour earthworms and fruit, however, and are unpleasant to handle.

Common black ground beetle
Pterostichus melanarius

FOR THE DEFENCE

Ground beetles are particularly valued for their appetite for slugs and snails, and will also consume millipedes, caterpillars, woodlice and more. Some will even eat aphids and small caterpillars.

FOR THE PROSECUTION

Extremely fond of eating small earthworms, ground beetles will munch on foliage and on strawberries and vegetable fruits such as tomatoes and cucumbers found on or near the soil surface. If handled they may eject a noxious, irritating fluid onto your skin.

THE TREATMENT

Mulch the soil under strawberries to prevent beetle attacks, but otherwise encourage these scavengers by providing shelter in compost heaps, log piles and the like. You might even consider installing or making 'beetle boxes' for overwinter protection.

Other helpful beetles

Ground beetles

Both ground beetles and their close relatives the rove beetles are welcome garden residents. They include:

 Snail hunter beetle (*Cychrus caraboides*): the adult feeds exclusively on snails; the larvae also eat slugs and other invertebrates. When threatened, they will squirt a noxious yellow acid from its abdomen.

 Bronze carabid beetle (*Carabus nemoralis*): feeds on slugs, snails, millipedes and the like; has a beautiful metallic sheen.

 Black clock beetle (*Pterostichus madidus*): nocturnal beetle that feeds on caterpillars, slugs and snails, but will eat foliage.

 Violet ground beetle (*Carabus violaceus*): superbly coloured consumer of slugs, snails, earthworms and insects.

Rove beetles (Family Staphylinidae)

Beetles with elongated bodies that are always on the move and often seen wandering on paths. Best known is the scorpion-like Devil's coach horse (*Ocypus olens*), named from the stink ejected from its abdomen, which it will raise when threatened.

Beetle lore

• It's said that if you stamp on a beetle it will rain the next time you hang washing out to dry.
• If a black beetle runs over your shoe, ill fortune will follow.
• In Ireland, it is bad luck to kill a Devil's coach horse, the 'punishment' being a physical injury. Reapers once put the beetles into their scythe handles to give them extra strength.
• In the Garden of Eden, the Devil's coach horse is said to have eaten the core of Eve's apple.

HONEYBEES

Family Apoidea

Apis mellifera

VERDICT

Honeybees are vital pollinators, easily encouraged into the garden by the flowers of both cultivated and weed species. Stings can be an occasional but sometimes serious hazard.

FOR THE DEFENCE

The essential pollination of plants takes place as honeybees forage for nectar and pollen. They are vital to the production of many garden crops, including fruits such as apples, plums and pears. The honey they make is our bonus.

FOR THE PROSECUTION

A bee sting is unpleasant. Treat one by pressing out the sting with a fingernail and applying ice or an antihistamine cream. If there are signs of anaphylaxis, such as swelling, nausea or vomiting, seek immediate medical attention.

THE TREATMENT

- Tempt bees into the garden with nectar and pollen rich flowers.
- Allow weeds such as clover, speedwell and dandelions to flower in lawns and other areas of the garden.
- Provide bees with the water essential for wax production.
- Don't use pesticides, even organic ones, except in extreme circumstances. Never, ever use them on or near open flowers.
- Avoid aggravating bees to prevent stings.
- Invite a neighbouring beekeeper to put one or more hives in your garden.

Floral choices

When selecting plants to provide maximum honeybee activity year round (see Good gardening practice) remember that:

- While honeybees only become active at 14°C, they will need sustenance if they emerge on warm winter days.

- Multipetalled varieties or those with double blooms are often inaccessible to bees. Simple is best.

- Blue and yellow flowers are most attractive to honeybees. A good scent like that of lavender will also help.

- Clumps of the same species planted together will assist foraging.

Would you believe it?

- Bees can detect ultraviolet light, which reveals to them the 'hidden' patterns on petals that have evolved to be particularly attractive to bees.
- Honeybees will collect resin from trees to make propolis, a substance vital for sterilizing the hive by killing bacteria (and useful for treating humans too).

- Pollen is used as a protein-rich food; most nectar is regurgitated for honey making.
- Bees in the hive tell each other where to find good flowers by means of a series of dances.
- Honeybees can sometimes make nests in garden tree trunks.

HOVERFLIES

Family Syrphidae

Bumblebee hoverfly *Volucella bombylans*

VERDICT

Among nature's great mimics, hoverflies are important pollinators. The larvae of most species feast on aphids and other insects, but some consume bulbs.

FOR THE DEFENCE

It is the aphid, caterpillar and mite consumption of their larvae that make hoverflies so valuable in the garden, along with the pollinating abilities of the adults. As long as birds can learn to distinguish hoverflies from the wasps and bees that hoverflies mimic, the adults are good to eat.

FOR THE PROSECUTION

The hoverflies most disliked by gardeners are those such as the large narcissus fly (*Merodon equestris*) which lays its eggs in all kinds of bulbs, from daffodils to snowdrops, leaving the hatched larvae an instantly accessible source of food. Other species' larvae will attack onion crops. The tic-tic or whining sound of a swarm of hoverflies can be disturbing.

THE TREATMENT

- **Listen for the whine of narcissus flies (bumblebee mimics) in late spring and early summer and swat as many as you can. Never use an insecticide.**
- **Attract hoverflies with a good selection of flowers.**
- **Leave weeds such as dandelions to flower to attract them.**
- **Make a pond.**

Survival strategies

Hoverflies take on a variety of forms and have remarkable powers that enable them to flourish.

The adult flies:

- Mimic wasps and bees but do not sting. As a bird or small mammal hesitates momentarily before attacking, the hoverfly escapes.
- Feed on pollen and nectar of many flowers.
- Possess small club-shaped gyroscopic organs called halteres which allow them to hover and feed for longer periods.

The larvae:
- Feed on the honeydew produced by aphids as well as the creatures themselves. In its two-week larval stage a single hoverfly grub can consume 800 aphids – many more than a ladybird.
- Larvae also eat rotting plant matter of all kinds.

  Some, despite being near blind, can detect aphids by scent alone.
- Water-dwelling larvae (rat-tailed maggots) have long, tubular tail ends that pierce the surface to take in vital oxygen.

Flowers to choose

Hoverflies are particularly attracted to yellow and orange flowers and, because of the specialized structure of their mouthparts, prefer simple and flat-topped species. Good choices include: achillea, alyssum, apple blossom, calendula, fennel, feverfew, French marigolds, helenium, hogweed, marsh marigold, michaelmas daisies and single-flowered dahlias.

LACEWINGS

Green lacewing *Chrysoperla carnea*

Order Neuroptera

VERDICT

Beautiful transparent-winged lacewings consume aphids by the thousand, plus other soft-bodied insects. Lacewings are also excellent pollinators. Both adults and larvae are important foods for birds and bats.

FOR THE DEFENCE

As well as devouring aphids, lacewing adults and larvae will help to rid the garden of scale insects, thrips, asparagus beetles and other pests. They are important pollinators, feeding on both pollen and nectar. Always encourage these superbly delicate insects, which fold their translucent, veined wings over their bodies like miniature tents when they are at rest.

FOR THE PROSECUTION

Lacewings are very rarely a problem, but have been known to transmit viral plant diseases. They will come into the house in winter.

THE TREATMENT

Attract lacewings to your garden by choosing plants with care. Excellent selections include yarrow, dill, fennel, coriander, the golden marguerite and cosmos. Dandelions are also beneficial, so let them survive and bloom where you can.

Because only a small proportion of lacewings will survive the winter unaided, help their prospects by buying (or making) and installing a lacewing chamber with its front set away from the prevailing wind. Replace the straw insert behind the louvred exterior every year.

Use lacewing larvae as a biological control for aphids – they can be bought ready to apply to the garden.

That's amazing!

- As it develops a single lacewing larva can eat as many as 10,000 aphids.

- If a mature lacewing lands on you it will almost certainly excrete onto you within seconds – hence its common name of stink fly. This happens because the larvae have no anuses. Their excrement is stored in their bodies until they metamorphose into adults.

- Lacewing larvae avoid detection from ants, birds and other predators by covering themselves with a camouflage made up of the dead bodies of aphids they have killed.

- The night-flying giant lacewings (*Osmylus fulvicephalus*) are the largest of Britain's species. Because their larvae are semi-aquatic, attract them with a garden pond.

- In the Harry Potter books, lacewings are used as an ingredient in magic potions.

- Lacewings are often aptly called golden eyes.

LADYBIRDS

Seven-spot ladybird *Coccinella 7-punctata*

Family Coccinellidae

VERDICT

The gardener's friend. Both adults and larvae of most British ladybird species devour aphids, although some are mildew and plant feeders. The immigrant Harlequin ladybird poses a threat to native species.

FOR THE DEFENCE

Arguably the prettiest insects in the garden (their colour is designed to warn off predators) adult ladybirds, with their variety of spot patterns on red or yellow backgrounds, can munch as many as 50 aphids a day while each larva consumes its own weight in aphids every 24 hours. In folklore, they are lucky, being said to hold the keys to heaven.

FOR THE PROSECUTION

The larger than 'normal' Harlequin ladybird, which arrived in Britain in 2004 and comes in a huge variety of colours and patterns, endangers the smaller, indigenous species. It competes with them for food and will even eat the eggs and larvae of native ladybirds as well as those of butterflies and moths. All ladybirds can bite, but insignificantly; they are more likely to deposit a smelly liquid on you.

TAKE CARE

If you want to keep your ladybirds never use insecticides. Even organic ones will destroy ladybirds and their larvae.

THE TREATMENT

There are many ways to encourage ladybirds to thrive in your garden.
• Collect any ladybirds hibernating indoors over winter. Store them in a cool place and release them in spring. Or buy and install ladybird 'houses' outdoors.
• Buy adults and larvae from a supplier and release them where most needed.
• You may wish to destroy any Harlequin ladybirds, but be sure to identify them correctly. Traditionally, to kill one is to bring bad luck.

What's in a name?

• The 'lady' in ladybird is the Virgin Mary, a connection first made in the Middle Ages. Its red colour represents Christ's blood or the red cloak of the Virgin depicted in some paintings. It is a 'bird' because it's regarded as a winged messenger, a kind of angel. Most prized is the 7-spot ladybird whose pattern portrays the mystic number – the seven joys and seven sorrows of the Virgin.
• Ladybird is an old term of endearment. The dozens of delightful common names for the ladybird include: Bishop barnabee, God's horse, God's little cow, Marygold, bushybandy, the Virgin's shoe and the blessing beetle.

LEAF-CUTTING BEES

Family Apidae

Leaf-cutting bee *Megachile* sp

VERDICT

These solitary bees cut semi-circular pieces out of leaves to line their nests made in any hollow cavity. They are important pollinators that favour cottage garden plants.

FOR THE DEFENCE

Key pollinators in the garden and beyond, leaf-cutter bees don't have pollen baskets on their legs, which means that as they carry pollen back to their nests much is spread around. Seeing a female carrying a piece of leaf back to the nest between her legs is a splendid sight. Their nests are unlikely to do any significant damage to brickwork.

FOR THE PROSECUTION

These bees have a special liking for rose leaves, making prize specimens look tatty. In late spring and all summer, they construct their nests in any convenient garden hollow – even in dry soil or in gaps in mortar. They will sting, but only when severely disturbed.

THE TREATMENT

Protect rose leaves from damage with a spray only as a very last resort. Otherwise encourage these bees by installing a 'bee box' composed of hollow pieces of wood to encourage nesting, or make one by enclosing dry stems such as hogweed or bamboo in a wooden frame or tin can.

Meet the relatives

Of all our bees, nine out of ten are solitary and all are essential pollinators. Following mating (after which the males die) females make the nests and lay individual eggs in enclosed cells in which they build pollen mounds glued together with nectar. Other solitary bees include:

Red mason bees (*Osmia bicornis*): reddish-ginger coloured bees favouring hollows in masonry for nesting.

Wood-carder bees (*Anthidium manicatum*): have distinctive yellow spots on the sides of their abdomens. Females 'comb' fibres from leaves; as they do so they are fiercely guarded by males waiting for potential mates.

Hairy-footed flower bees (*Anthophora plumipes*): look like bumblebees; nest in groups in soil and soft mortar.

Tawny mining bees (*Andrena fulva*): gingery bees that make volcano-like mounds of earth at their burrow entrances.

Bees beware!

Solitary bees are assiduous in sealing their nests but may still fall prey to 'cuckoo' parasites – species of bee, wasp, beetle and fly that invade ready-made nests and use them for egg-laying. The eggs of the solitary bee, or hatched larvae, are invariably eaten in the process.

LEATHERJACKETS

Family Tipulidae

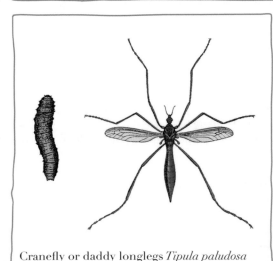

Cranefly or daddy longlegs *Tipula paludosa*

VERDICT

Leatherjackets – cranefly larvae – can ruin a lawn by feeding on grass roots. Damage is exacerbated by the starlings and other birds that relish them. The adults are efficient pollinators.

FOR THE DEFENCE

It is as bird food that leatherjackets are most admirable, despite the problems they can cause. They are particularly important for starlings, whose populations are in decline (see Birds). Craneflies eat pollen, dispersing it in the process, and also feed on decaying plant matter, helping the garden nutrient cycle. Bats enjoy craneflies as part of their nocturnal diet.

Many names

Among the many descriptive names given to craneflies are: harry-long-legs, granny knobble-knees, meggie nettles (because they were once thought to sting), meggie spinner, spinning jennie and tom-taylor.

A lawn plagued with leatherjackets develops nasty yellow-brown patches that can become completely bare. Starlings – often in big flocks – plus jackdaws, rooks and magpies will make holes in the grass as they feed hungrily on these tough-skinned legless grubs. Foxes, hedgehogs and badgers will also dig for them. Leatherjackets will also feed on seedling roots, leading to a swift collapse and death. The adults, with their haphazard flight, can worry some people especially when they appear in profusion in late summer and autumn.

THE TREATMENT

- **Keep your lawn in maximum health by feeding it well and scarifying it to remove dead grass and moss.**
- **Test for leatherjackets by soaking the grass with water, then covering it with black polythene overnight. The leatherjackets will come to the surface.**
- **Between August and October, water well, then apply a *Steinernema carpocapsae* nematode treatment, being sure to treat the edges of infested areas.**
- **If a lawn is very badly affected, remove all the grass, treat the leatherjackets and resow or returf.**

Secrets of success

- Leatherjackets can overwinter. If the weather is mild they will start causing problems in late winter or early spring. In a cold winter they will hibernate, but begin eating roots by early to mid summer.

- Fully grown leatherjackets pupate in the soil, ready for adults to emerge in August, when they mate and lay eggs.

- A cranefly's legs act as balancers, but it can exist without the full complement. Legs are often lost from being caught in spiders' webs.

LILY BEETLES

Scarlet lily beetle *Lilioceris lilii*

Family Chrysomelidae

VERDICT

Both bright red adult lily beetles and their larvae can decimate lilies and their relations and are hard to control, especially organically. They are most active between March and October.

FOR THE DEFENCE

Zoologically speaking, it is hard not to admire these beetles' spectacular colouring which, along with their ability to squeak when touched, deters bird predators. Their sheer success as garden pests is a marvel. Don't confuse lily beetles with cardinal beetles which are twice as big (up to 16 mm/⅓ in long), feed solely on insects, and reside mostly on tree trunks.

Lilies of all kinds, plus fritillaries and nomocharis, are prey to lily beetle attacks, causing such damage that below ground bulbs are so severely affected that they will fail to flower the next season. The reddish brown larvae, which disguise themselves with their own blackish excrement, begin by feeding on leaf undersides; as they age they devour complete leaves. The adults munch rounded holes in leaves before moving on to eat the petals and seedpods. They overwinter in leaf debris or in the soil ready to mate and lay eggs the following spring.

THE TREATMENT

By hand:
• **Check vulnerable plants frequently from early spring until autumn and rub off and destroy any lozenge shaped orange-red eggs, red-brown larvae or bright red adults you find.**
Using pesticides:
• **These are most effective on the larvae but never use them on plants that are in flower.**
• **Always read the label.**
• **For an organic pesticide, use one containing natural pyrethrins.**
• **Non-organic choices are between those with artificial pyrethrins or those containing acetamiprid. (See Pesticides and how to use them.)**

Beware the beetles

In spring, following mating, each female lily beetle lays between 200 and 300 eggs which hatch into larvae in just a week.

Lily beetles reached Britain from the Mediterranean in the early 1900s but only became a problem from 1940 when the first one was spotted in a garden in Cobham, Surrey.

Scientists working on biological controls have discovered larvae of parasitic wasps feeding on lily beetle grubs which may lead to a new, effective treatment.

MILLIPEDES

Spotted snake millipede *Blaniulus guttulatus*

Class Diplopoda

VERDICT

Although some millipedes can damage soft foliage, fruit and underground plant structures, all are invaluable recyclers of plant material in the garden and good food for favoured garden residents.

FOR THE DEFENCE

As nature's efficient decomposers and recyclers, millipedes break down all kinds of organic matter to release valuable nutrients and benign bacteria into the soil. They are excellent food for hedgehogs, frogs, toads and ground beetles, and make easy pickings for all kinds of birds.

FOR THE PROSECUTION

Millipedes, which have quite weak mouthparts, are most likely to exacerbate the damage already done to bulbs, roots and tubers (especially potatoes) by creatures such as slugs or other soil-living pests. Strawberries are also vulnerable, as are seedlings of all kinds. They can sometimes multiply very quickly, creating hungry 'swarms' which can be particularly attractive to starlings.

THE TREATMENT

Getting rid of slugs is the best way to control millipede damage to crops such as potatoes. Setting straw or hay under ripening strawberries will also help. Keep seedlings well (but not over) watered to promote strength and decrease their vulnerability.

Encourage millipedes with a healthy, well-constructed compost heap that allows them easy access.

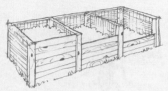

Did you know?

- Millipedes rarely have more than 50 feet – certainly not a thousand.
- They were once used medicinally to help kidney function and, as a powder, rubbed on the body to remove excess hair.
- When threatened, millipedes produce an array of toxic chemicals which deter some, but certainly not all their predators.
- Galley worms, coach and horses and thrush lice are alternative millipede names.

Meet the relatives

There are 64 species of millipedes in Britain and Ireland including:
• Pill millipedes or 'rollers' which can curl up like woodlice.
• The many-legged Julida group of millipedes, which are supreme tunnellers. The blunt-tailed snake millipede has about 200 legs.
• The flat-backed millipedes or 'wedgers', adept at pushing through cracks. When picked up they release a weak cyanide compound smelling of bitter almonds that can kill other invertebrates.

SAWFLIES

Apple sawfly *Hoplocampa testudinea*

Suborder Symphyta

VERDICT

A range of wasp-like species. Sawfly larvae devastate the foliage of the particular plants on which they are adapted to feed, but are excellent food for many birds and other garden residents.

FOR THE DEFENCE

Adult sawflies are not only excellent pollinators but feature widely in the diets of frogs, toads and birds as well as ants and spiders. The larvae are particularly relished by birds. Sawfly attack is rarely fatal to plants, most are able to survive and regrow their foliage in the same or subsequent year.

FOR THE PROSECUTION

Sawfly species are adapted to feed on plants and crops such as apples, roses and gooseberries. As well as stripping the foliage of affected plants right down to the ribs, sawfly larvae, which look like caterpillars, can severely damage apples. Cropping of gooseberries can also be severely reduced. Affected plants (see opposite) look extremely unsightly.

THE TREATMENT

- Encourage birds into the garden by setting vulnerable plants in open positions.
- Look regularly from April onwards for tell-tale signs of egg laying such as greyish translucent patches on leaves and elongated greyish 'scars' on stems or leaf stalks. Cut off any badly affected parts.
- Inspect vulnerable plants regularly and pick off any larvae by hand.
- Use an organic insecticide such as pyrethrum, but never when nearby plants are in flower.

Sawfly hosts

The sawflies whose larvae most commonly affect garden plants include:

- Apple sawfly (*Hoplocampa testudinea*): also attacks cherries and plums. Larvae develop inside the fruit, causing severe damage.

- Gooseberry sawfly (*Nematus ribesii*): also attacks currants. Strips leaves and reduces berry formation.

- Pear and cherry 'slugworm' (*Caliroa cerasi*): also attacks cotoneaster, chaenomeles (japonica) and sorbus making leaves dry up and turn brown.

- Large rose sawfly (*Arge ochropus*): defoliates plants. Roses are also affected by the rose-leaf rolling sawfly and the rose slug sawfly.

And ...

Other plants that can be affected include Solomon's seal, aquilegia, goat's beard, iris, mallow, berberis and hibiscus.

How sawflies behave

The success of sawflies is linked to many aspects of their behaviour, including:
- Adult females literally saw into plant tissue before inserting their eggs into the cuts.

- When disturbed, the larvae, which feed in groups, distract predators by curling into S-shapes and raising their rear ends.
- Two or three generations are produced in a single growing season.

SCALE INSECTS

Soft scale *Coccus hesperidum*

Family Coccidae

VERDICT

Two types of insect – soft and armoured scale insects – suck the sap of many plants, stunting their growth, and many excrete sticky honeydew. They are a food relished by ladybirds and lacewings.

FOR THE DEFENCE

Ladybirds and lacewings, both of which are important in helping to control garden pests, will eat large quantities of scale insects. They are taken by some small birds.

Insects with history

- Some scholars believe that the manna eaten by Moses and the Israelites during the Exodus was scale insect honeydew.
- The red dye cochineal produced by scale insects was once used to colour the coats of the British army.
- Natural shellac, a tough resin, is made by Asian scale insect species.

Plant stems and leaf undersides affected by these insects – which include fruit trees (especially figs), lilac, bay, ivy and ferns – develop patches of unsightly scales or lumps. As their sap is 'stolen', plants die back or become stunted or fail to thrive. Eggs can be laid enclosed in a mass of waxy white fibres. Once mature, the insects never move their positions, and cling on even after death – the scales are their corpses. The sweet honeydew deposited on plants can encourage colonization by sooty moulds.

THE TREATMENT

Because of their waxy outer coverings, scale insects respond poorly to pesticides, so other methods of control need trying before you resort to non-organic solutions such as acetamiprid (see Pesticides and how to use them). Vigilance is key.
• Rub off any eggs as soon as you see them.
• Look out for soft-bodied yellow-orange 'crawlers', the intermediate stages in the life cycles of armoured scale insects. Because these don't cling on tightly, success with an organic pesticide such as natural pyrethrum or plant oils is possible, but several applications will be necessary.
• Try a biological control containing the nematodes *Steinernema feltiae*.

Fungal opportunists

When camellias, rhododendrons, holly, yew and other evergreens are attacked by cushion scale (a soft type), infestation by black sooty moulds invariably follows during winter and into spring. Upper surfaces of leaves are most commonly affected, but eggs, lying dormant over the winter will usually be found on their undersides. Plants will be weakened if the unsightly mould blocks out light, preventing good photosynthesis.

SLUGS

Great black slug *Arion ater*

Family Limacidae

VERDICT

Rightly loathed by gardeners, and hard to control, slugs munch all manner of plant material, including foliage, fruit and bulbs. But they are essential food for hedgehogs, birds and other creatures.

FOR THE DEFENCE

Slugs are important to the diets of hedgehogs, frogs, toads, slowworms, ground beetles and other beneficial garden creatures. Birds that enjoy them include blackbirds, thrushes, robins and owls. They also help significantly in consuming dead and rotting vegetation.

FOR THE PROSECUTION

From hostas and cyclamens to lettuces, tomatoes and onions, there are dozens of garden plants prone to slug attack. Ironically it is the smallest ones that do the most damage. Slugs will attract some less welcome birds such as starlings, crows and gulls into the garden.

THE TREATMENT

- Choose slug resistant species and varieties when possible.
- Water on a nematode worm biological control. Use slug pellets only as a last resort and choose organic ones labelled as containing ferric phosphate. (See Pesticides and how to use them). Aside from going out at night with a torch to seize and kill offenders, there are many ways to deter and trap slugs, most of which will also work for snails (see Insects and other Invertebrates). These include:
- Upturned empty grapefruit halves with holes cut into them are good, but can look unsightly.
- Beer traps (shallow beer-filled containers) in which slugs will drown are effective but unattractive. They need constant maintenance.
- Gravel and glass chippings over which slugs dislike moving can be effective, but you may need them in large quantities.
- Coffee grounds spread around plants may or may not work, but are worth trying.
- Plastic bottles can be used to cover individual plants.
- Copper rings placed around plants in pots may stop slugs from climbing.

That's sluggish!

🐌 To be sluggish is to be slow. Measurements suggest that the farthest most slugs could travel in a day is 200 m (218 yards).

🐌 That a slug is a term for a bullet probably links to the shapes they share.

🐌 Slugs have many alternative names including dew snails, naked snails, slimeys, marly-sarlies and mollscrolls.

🐌 Slugs were once boiled in milk and administered as a medicine to cure consumption (tuberculosis).

SNAILS

Garden snail *Cornu aspersum* (formerly *Helix aspersa*)

Class Gastropoda

VERDICT

Shelled molluscs that munch mainly on plant tissues, snails leave their trails on garden paths and plants. They are an important food for many garden creatures and essential to the nutrient cycle.

FOR THE DEFENCE

Soft snail bodies feature in the diets of birds, notably thrushes, but blue and great tits will peck at partially degraded shells to obtain the calcium they need for eggshell production. Snails help to clean up the garden by eating rotting leaves, dung and even slug and snail corpses. Small rodents like wood mice, plus frogs, toads, hedgehogs and ground beetles all depend on snails for survival.

Although they normally feed near the ground, where they can reduce soft-leaved seedlings to zero, snails are capable, both day and night (but especially in wet weather) of gliding up tall plants to eat holes in their leaves or to consume soft fruit, including tomatoes. They hide in dark damp places under plants and on walls. And snail trails can mar the looks of prize plants. Except in the depths of winter, snails will mate and lay eggs all year.

THE TREATMENT

It is impossible to eradicate snails from the garden but it is vital to protect vulnerable plants from damage as you would for slugs (see Insects and other Invertebrates). More specific anti-snail measures include:
• By torchlight, collect snails into a sealable plastic bag. Release them in a well-vegetated site a good distance away. Or squash them and dump them onto the compost heap.
• In winter, collect hibernating snails and treat them as above.
• Leave crushed or empty shells in the garden for birds to eat and for other invertebrates such as mining bees to nest in.

Did you know?

- Snails can 'home' and will return to your garden if taken or thrown less than 20 m (60 ft) from where you found them.
- During World War II, garden snails were eaten in times of food shortages. The smaller, banded snails are much less damaging than 'regular' ones.
- Snail racing is a centuries old sport.

A good sign

If you see collections of broken, empty snail shells near stones in the garden then you are almost certainly lucky enough to have a thrush's 'anvil'. Keep watch and you should see the bird at work.

SOCIAL WASPS

Common wasp or jasper *Vespula vulgaris*

Family Vespidae

VERDICT

Although they are sting-dealing nuisances, especially in late summer and early autumn, wasps are important consumers of grubs and caterpillars and can act as pollinators. They make superbly architectural nests.

FOR THE DEFENCE

Worker (female) wasps work in groups to cut up and eat caterpillars, such as those of the cabbage white (see Insects and other Invertebrates), which are anathema to gardeners. They also eat flies, aphids and a wide range of other invertebrates – both alive and dead. Wasps will help to transfer pollen from plant to plant and are a favourite food for spiders.

FOR THE PROSECUTION

The sting of a wasp, especially if inflicted on the face, neck or scalp, can produce a severe allergic reaction known as anaphylactic shock, which needs immediate medical attention. Unlike bees, wasps do not die after stinging. Wasps are notoriously drawn to the sweet foods, including apples, pears and plums. Any windfalls become instant wasp attractants.

THE TREATMENT

• If a wasp's nest is a problem, call your local authority to deal with it. Do not remove it yourself.
• Deter wasps with a pheromone trap – wasps are drawn to the chemicals that mimic those of their own kind (see Biological controls).
• Avoid using insecticides if at all possible.

Skills and needs

The queen wasp begins building her nest in spring. First she feeds on nectar and pollen for energy, then uses wood chewed from plants (and even garden furniture and sheds) to construct up to 30 papery cells in which she lays her first batch of eggs, covering the first part of her construction with a natural ant-repelling chemical. As eggs hatch, more cells are added.

Worker wasps feed the larvae with high protein animal food – caterpillars, grubs and the like – and are rewarded with the drops of sugary nectar secreted by the larvae. By late summer, however, there are few larvae remaining, which explains why the wasps need to get their sugar 'fix' from other sources such as picnics.

A bigger relation

The hornet (*Vespa crabro*) is much larger than the common wasp, measuring up to 3 cm (1¼ in) long. Contrary to popular belief, hornets very rarely sting, but if you kill a hornet the pheromones released can trigger all the occupants of a nest to fly out and attack you.

SPIDERS

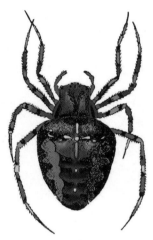

Cross spider *Araneus diadematus*

Order Arachnida

VERDICT

Impressive, vigilant insect eaters, and food for a wide range of welcome garden inhabitants, but spiders also consume useful species. Spiders can provoke debilitating phobias in some people.

FOR THE DEFENCE

Not only will the spider's web put an end to unwanted insects including pestiferous beetles, but spiders will also eat earwigs, millipedes and occasionally aphids. Spiders are important members of the garden ecosystem, providing food for a wide range of creatures from birds to hedgehogs, frogs and toads.

FOR THE PROSECUTION

Spiders' webs are not appreciated by the tidiest gardeners, and the insect diet of garden spiders can include useful pollinators including bees. When picked up, some spiders, including the cross spider, can inflict nasty bites. The presence of spiders is more than unpleasant to anyone with arachnophobia.

THE TREATMENT

The best treatment for spiders is to interfere as little as possible in their lives. Don't tidy the garden – or your shed – too much to give them adequate shelter over the winter and resist removing their webs.

Spidery facts

- Britain is home to around 650 species of spider.
- On average a single spider will eat two insects a month for six months of the year – but a large garden can contain over a million spiders!
- The females spin the webs and coat their feet with oil to prevent themselves sticking to their own silk.
- Spiders are particularly active in autumn because this is when mating takes place and eggs are produced.

- Young spiders or spiderlings hatch en masse in spring from up to 800 eggs laid in an egg sac.
- The female spider uses her silk to protect her young as well as for web building.

Myth, legend and superstition

- Arachnids, the zoological group that includes spiders are named from the Greek girl Arachne, renowned for her spinning and weaving skills, who was changed into a spider by her jealous rival the goddess Athene.
- In West African legend, the spider is a supreme trickster Anansi.

- It's said that 'If in life you want to thrive/Let a spider run alive'.
- A spider's web on a boat is believed to prevent it from sinking.
- As long as a spider stays calmly in its web then the weather will be similarly stable – and sunny.

THRIPS OR THUNDER FLIES

Onion thrip *Thrips tabaci*

Order Thysanoptera

VERDICT

Minute, feathery-winged, swarming insects thrips suck the sap from a variety of flowers and vegetables and feed on dead vegetation. They are enjoyed by birds.

FOR THE DEFENCE

Thrips are a particularly important food for swallows and house martins that feed on the wing.

FOR THE PROSECUTION

Leaves attacked by thrips develop mottled patches as the insects scrape away the surface to reach the nutritious sap. They can also develop a silvery surface discolouration bearing tiny black spots of insect excrement. Alternatively brown mottled patches can appear. Flower buds affected by thrips fail to open and petals become mottled and stained. They will also ruin bulbs. Thrip bites are mildly irritating and have been known to transmit viral diseases.

THE TREATMENT

• **Where possible, hang up sticky traps to attract the insects. Try blue as well as yellow ones.**
• **Use an organic insecticide such as one based on pyrethrum or plant oil but remember that it will kill other insects too.**
• **Use a biological control containing predatory mites that will eat the larvae. These are supplied in sachets to hang on plants.**
• **Remove and destroy damaged foliage or flower buds as soon as possible to allow plants to generate new growth.**

Common thrips

Outdoors, the most common garden thrips are:

- Gladiolus thrips: also feed on freesias and can overwinter in corms and bulbs.
- Pea thrips: discolour pods and prevent peas developing within. Whole plants may be stunted.
- Privet thrips: also attack lilac, discolouring foliage.
- Onion thrips: feed on other family members, particularly leeks, but also on cucumbers, tomatoes, carnations, chrysanthemums, begonias and dahlias.
- Honeysuckle thrips: can also attack other garden flowers.

WARNING!
Never spray plants in flower to get rid of thrips – you will kill vital pollinators.

Would you believe it?

• The word thrips comes from the Greek for woodlouse; they are also called tassle-wings, storm flies, corn lice and harvest bugs.
• Swarms are most common in warm, damp weather.
• They find their way indoors, notably behind picture frames.
• One thrip can lay up to 100 eggs directly onto a plant. Its entire life cycle lasts only 24 to 35 days.

V

VINE WEEVILS

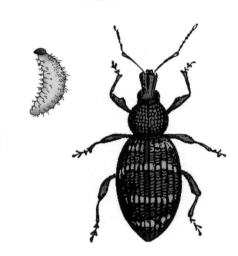

Vine weevil *Otiorhynchus sulcatus*

Family Curculionidae

VERDICT

Adult vine weevils nibble leaf edges but it is their larvae that can do lethal damage to ornamental plants of all kinds, particularly those grown in pots and/or the greenhouse.

FOR THE DEFENCE

Both adults and larvae are a feast for birds, hedgehogs, frogs and toads, and for a variety of beetles, which makes them essential components of the garden ecosystem. Like many invertebrates it is difficult not to admire them for their successful survival strategies.

FOR THE PROSECUTION

Vine weevil larvae – shining white grubs with brown heads, measuring about 1 cm (¹/₃ in) long and curled in half moons – literally suck the life out of plants, making leaves turn a reddish colour, droop and fall. Strawberries, polyanthus, heucheras and sedums are particularly vulnerable, the more so if they are grown in pots where warmth and dampness are great attractions (the risk increases massively in the greenhouse). Below the soil surface, grubs burrow into the tubers of cyclamens and begonias. Foliage favoured by the adult insects includes that of rhododendrons, hydrangeas, chrysanthemums, bergenias, and strawberries.

THE TREATMENT

- **Use your eyes. Look out for the larvae, especially under the rims of pots and in autumn and winter where they can accumulate ready to strike at plant roots. Pick them off and squash them.**
- **Search the garden at night with a torch for active adults and dispatch them too. Shake shrub branches over a sheet to help dislodge them.**
- **Clear up garden debris in which the creatures can breed.**
- **Use a biological control containing nematodes which can be watered onto the garden using the manufacturer's instructions. It needs to be refrigerated.**
- **As a last resort, use a chemical pesticide.**
- **Destroy damaged plants.**
- **Sterilize pots or containers before reusing them.**
- **Encourage natural predators in the garden.**

Worst weevils

In history, the worst weevil damage was that of the boll or cotton weevil which in the 1920s brought the American cotton industry to its knees. However the infestation resulted in agricultural divergence away from cotton dependency in the South, and the weevil is celebrated in Enterprise, Alabama. Long before this, the grain weevil robbed humans of their harvest in ancient Rome and in 12th century England.

WIREWORMS

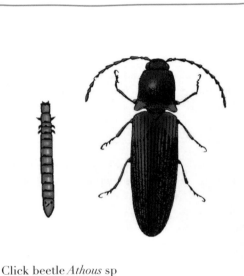

Click beetle *Athous* sp

Family Elateridae

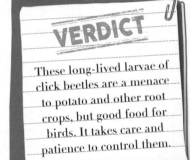

VERDICT

These long-lived larvae of click beetles are a menace to potato and other root crops, but good food for birds. It takes care and patience to control them.

FOR THE DEFENCE

Birds feed happily on wireworms as long as they are brought to the surface, and are particularly relished in winter, when other food is often scarce.

FOR THE PROSECUTION

Wireworms, with their unmistakable squirming, shiny orange-yellow bodies and three pairs of short legs, can render a crop of potatoes, carrots or beetroot impossible to store for the winter – or even totally inedible. They can also damage lawns and ornamental grasses.

THE TREATMENT

Be aware of the click beetle lifecycle to help control wireworms.
• **Grow early varieties and/or lift crops before September. After cropping, remove all crop traces, especially 'miniature' potatoes.**
• **Try burying some 'traps'. Once crops start to swell, push halved potatoes onto sticks and bury them 5 to 10 cm (2 to 4 in) deep. Pull them up, dispose of the wireworms and replace them every two weeks.**
• **Dig the soil well in winter to expose adults and larvae; turn the compost heap regularly.**
• **Grow a green manure such as mustard alongside crops in late summer to attract wireworms.**
• **Rotate crops – plant peas and beans that will be unaffected in wireworm infested areas.**
• **Apply a nematode based biological control.**

That's amazing!

- A single click beetle can lay 250 eggs.
- An adult click beetle can jump to 30 cm (1 ft) at a speed of 2.5 m (8 ft) per second. As it jumps it can turn up to six somersaults.
- The loud click comes from a special peg in the joint between thorax and abdomen which is released as the creature flicks upwards.
- When disturbed, beetles will lie on their backs and feign death, but can jump even from a 'legs up' position.

The beetle lifecycle

Essential year-round knowledge to help prevent problems.
April to June: adults begin feeding just below the soil surface, then mate.
May to June: eggs are laid and hatch into larvae.
June to September: larvae feed on roots and other vegetation.
September to October: fully grown larvae pupate, but this can be delayed for up to five years.
October to April: adults and larvae overwinter in the soil.

WOODLICE

Common or rough woodlouse
Porcellio scaber

Order Isopoda

VERDICT

Remarkable land-living crustaceans, woodlice are nature's ardent, efficient recyclers and essential to any compost heap. Woodlice do little or no damage to living plants.

FOR THE PROSECUTION

Woodlice can occasionally feed on soft young vegetation or strawberries unprotected from direct contact with the soil. Because they excrete ammonia through pores in their external skeletons, they have a distinctive unpleasant smell.

FOR THE DEFENCE

An abundance of woodlice is a sign of a healthy garden in which dead organic matter is recycled to make nutrients available to growing plants. They feed mostly on damp plant material that is beginning to decompose including rotting wood, leaf litter, windfall fruit, dead animals and even their own faeces.

THE TREATMENT

Encourage woodlice by making sure that your garden isn't too clean and tidy. Even if you don't have a compost heap, collect fallen leaves and prunings and make them into piles where woodlice can feed and reproduce.

More good points

- Since they first evolved some 500 million years ago, woodlice have changed very little.

- At night, when woodlice emerge to feed, many other garden creatures dine on them, including toads, shrews, centipedes and beetles.

- Woodlice are unappetizing to young birds, but adults will crunch them up to help obtain the calcium they need for making eggshells.

- Woodlice consume their own faeces to obtain copper, a metal key to the composition of their blood.

- In Medieval times woodlice mixed with wine were administered to relieve symptoms of bladder and urinary tract disorders.

In a ball

Pill bugs or pill woodlice (*Armadillidium vulgare*), also known as little armadillos, have the fascinating ability to roll themselves into balls when touched or threatened.

Many names

Woodlice have dozens of nicknames.
- Many, such as fuzzy-pig, journey-pig, sow-bug, sowpig, hog louse, wood pig and tiggy-hog, are based on their reputation as effective little scavengers.
- From their shoe-like shape they are dubbed shoemakers.

- They are called slaters from their ability to live under loose roof slates.
- Rolling up in balls is the origin of names such as cheese-bob, roll-in-balls and roly-poly.
- Pissibeds originates from their ammonia, urine-like smell.

Dealing
with
Wildlife

To encourage a healthy garden community it is important to garden well, and to be aware of the effects your actions may have. These include the keeping of cats, dogs and other domestic animals, the actions of pesticides and your legal obligations in relation to wildlife. Complete with a list of good plants to grow to encourage pollinators and other wildlife into your garden, these pages will help to enhance your knowledge in combination with the individual entries included in the book.

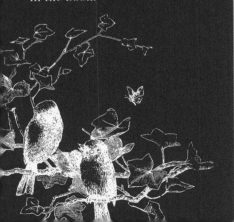

GOOD GARDENING PRACTICE

By gardening well, it is certainly possible to control or even eliminate garden pests without resorting to chemical controls of any kind.

GENERAL CARE
Healthy plants will be best equipped to cope with pest attacks. This includes making sure your soil is well manured. Other key actions include:
- In the vegetable garden, rotate crops to help prevent repeat infestations of pests such as wireworms and eelworms.
- Prune plants regularly to stimulate healthy growth and deadhead routinely to promote maximum flowering.
- Delay cutting back perennials until the spring to provide shelter for animals over the winter.
- Choose pest resistant varieties.
- Select plants that will attract insects and birds, especially beneficial insects such as hoverflies and lacewings.
- Provide water for pollinators and for birds and mammals.
- Try companion planting, using plants to help ward off pests.
- Experiment with different planting schedules to help avoid the times of year when specific pests are most active.
- Keep weeds under control but leave those

such as dandelions, buttercups and clover to flower where you can to help attract a wide range of pollinators.

• Grow plants that will give shelter and provide bedding and nesting materials for creatures you wish to encourage.

• Have a year-round log pile that can provide cover.

• Remove all rubbish that can attract unwanted scavengers such as rats, crows and foxes.

• Avoid using glyphosate weed killers which can harm animals that feed on vegetation.

Barriers, traps and deterrents

Use physical barriers to pests and unwelcome visitors whenever possible. These can be anything from prickly hedges to fencing, netting or fleece.

• Use textured mulches, varying from woodchips to gravel.

• Pick pests off plants by hand (use a torch at night) or try washing them off with a hose.

• Protect individual plants with plastic bottles.

• Use beer traps, grapefruit halves and other physical traps to catch pests such as slugs.

• Hang up sticky yellow or blue traps.

• Deter birds and larger animals with shiny objects or scarecrows. Sound-based devices and

movement-triggered garden lights can also work.

Repellents

Denying pests access to plants is an excellent means of control. As well as those recommended for slugs and snails (see Insects and other Invertebrates) it is easy to mix your own repellents in the kitchen. Good examples are:

Garlic spray Purée the cloves of 2 garlic bulbs in a food processor with a little water. Stir this into 1 litre of water. Leave for 1–2 hours, then strain. Optionally, add a teaspoon of liquid soap.

Chilli pepper spray Mix 1 tablespoon of chilli (cayenne pepper) powder with 1 litre of water and a teaspoon of liquid soap.

COMPANION PLANTING

Companion plants will deter unwanted creatures or attract them in preference to your favourites. Many companion plants not only look good in the garden but have the bonus of assisting pollination, while others are chosen to be deliberate sacrifices to hungry pests. If you can, set them interspersed between crops for best effect.

Good choices of companion plants include:
• Chives, onions and their relations (*Allium* spp): have a strong scent that will deter aphids.
• English marigolds (*Calendula officinalis*): can lure aphids away from beans and repel whitefly. Attractive to ladybirds, lacewings and hoverflies.
• Fennel (*Foeniculum vulgare*): flowers attract aphid-eating hoverflies.
• French marigolds (*Tagetes patula*): sacrificial plants that will lure slugs away from hostas and other vulnerable plants.
• Lavender (*Lavandula angustifolia*): deters aphids and attracts bees, hoverflies and other pollinators.
• Mint (*Mentha spicata*): deters flea beetles and (to an extent) carrot fly.
• Nasturtiums (*Tropaeolum majus*):

sacrificial plant that tempts aphids of all kind, so protecting beans and brassicas.
• Sage (*Salvia officinalis*) Attracts bees and hoverflies with its strong scent which also repels pests prone to damaging brassicas.
• Summer savoury (*Satureja hortensis*): a lure for blackfly, best planted among broad beans and roses.
• Thyme (*Thymus vulgaris*): has a strong scent to help deter blackfly and other aphids from roses.
• Wormwood (*Artemisia absinthium*): attractive highly scented foliage deters aphids and flea beetles. The yellow flowers attract hoverflies, lacewings and ladybirds.
• Yarrow (*Achillea millefolium*): best near brassicas, tomatoes, spinach and melons to attract pollinators and aphid-eaters.

BIOLOGICAL CONTROLS

For some garden problems biological controls can reduce or even do away with the need for pesticides. Targeted at specific pests, new ones are constantly being developed. As a general rule:
• Follow the suppliers' instructions to the letter, including temperature and time storage specifications.
• Use alone, not mixed with any chemical pesticides.
• Apply them as early as possible when a problem develops.

Biological controls are sold by specialist garden centres but more usually available by mail order. The main types are:

Nematodes Species of worms that enter the bodies of other invertebrates, including slugs, carrot fly, wireworms and leatherjackets where they release deadly bacteria. They work best in a moist environment, so are generally watered on; most will work well above 12°C. Check suitability before you buy. (See individual entries for specific recommendations.)

Mites Predatory mites will work to combat thrips and spider mites.

Parasitic wasps These wasps lay eggs in the bodies of pests; the larvae that develop feed on and kill them. They can control cabbage white butterflies and, particularly, aphids in greenhouses.

Hoverfly, lacewing and ladybird larvae can be applied to feed on pests. They are particularly effective against aphids.

PHEROMONE TRAPS

These traps work by using the powerful hormones made by fertile female moths, butterflies and other insects to lure and trap males, so reducing mating and subsequently the number of eggs laid – and caterpillars hatched. They are particularly useful in helping to control codling moths and cutworms.

DOMESTICATED WILDLIFE

They may not technically be classed as 'wildlife' but pets and domesticated birds have significant impacts on the garden and its ecosystem.

CATS

Their predatory inheritance makes it inevitable that cats will chase and kill small creatures. Even in the daytime, but most often if allowed to roam at night, they will hunt down mice, voles and slowworms, often bringing them as dead or dying offerings. Small birds, especially the young and injured, are also feline victims, but most cats will shrink when confronted by a hedgehog or a pheasant. The other chief problem with cats is their habit of digging and defaecating in garden soil.

Some good ways of deterring cats include:

Mulching and ground cover Deter digging with soil mulched with wood chips, pine cones, or gravel, or planted with groundcover plants.

Scent and touch Strong smelling plants, including lemon balm, rue, lavender, curry plants and geraniums will deter some cats. Many gardeners swear by the annual *Coleus canina* dubbed the 'scaredy-cat' or 'pee-off' plant. Cats also dislike prickly plants such as holly, blackberries and blackthorn which are good hedge choices.

Litter box An outdoor litter box, 'baited' with catnip (*Nepeta* sp) planted nearby can help to keep cats off beds and borders.

Water and sound A hand or automated waterpistol can scare away cats, as can ultrasonic repellents.

DOGS

Because it contains high levels of nitrogen, dog urine can damage a lawn, scorching the grass. Bitches pose the most problems because, unlike males, they urinate on one spot rather than depositing small amounts in a variety of places. Dog-owning gardeners also need to avoid plants that are poisonous to dogs if eaten. If your garden is visited by badgers, foxes or hedgehogs beware of aggressive canine confrontations.

Some solutions to canine problems include:

Training and aftercare Dogs can be trained to avoid urinating on the lawn but if they do, apply plenty of water as soon as possible.

Landscaping and planting Consider

replacing grass with harder landscaping. Use prickly plants to create more impenetrable garden borders. All the scented plants recommended for deterring cats (see left) can also work to discourage dogs.

Plants to avoid Check out a full list of plants poisonous to dogs. These include azaleas, cyclamen, daffodil bulbs, delphiniums, hyacinths, hydrangeas, laburnum, lily of the valley, lupins, rhododendrons and wisteria.

CHICKENS

Eating fresh eggs from your own chickens is a delight, but their care needs balancing with that of the rest of the garden. They will devour slugs in quantity, and you can feed them beetles and cabbage white caterpillars, but they will take and enjoy earthworms, eat newly sown seeds and root up seedlings, take dust baths in freshly dug or dry soil and peck at tomatoes and soft fruit. Hens can easily fall prey to foxes.

Balance your needs as poultry keeper and gardener in these ways.

Fencing Keep chickens confined to a specific area. Low fencing arches around beds and borders are effective deterrents.

Mulching Use flat stones around plants and, on larger areas, plastic sheeting or old blankets.

Protection Keep vulnerable plants covered with well-pegged netting or fleece. Or plant them in raised beds.

DUCKS

Ducks are easy to keep if you have enough space. They eat many more slugs, snails and other unwelcome garden vertebrates than chickens, and have little appetite for garden plants, but they are partial to lettuce and strawberries and can trample and destroy seedlings. Water is essential, as is night-time shelter. You will need to keep ducks confined as for chickens, but they can, of course, escape on the wing.

GEESE

A large open, informal space is ideal for geese, which feed almost exclusively on grass – and on which they will defaecate messily. They also favour high-protein clover. An orchard is excellent for geese. Their noisiness makes geese renowned as 'guard dogs' but they can peck at children allowed to approach them unsupervised. They need to be fenced in, not least for protection from badgers and foxes.

PESTICIDES AND HOW TO USE THEM

Whether home-made, organic or synthetic, pesticides should always be regarded as a last resort. That is because a pesticide will kill indiscriminately, dealing death to pollinators and other beneficial species, as well as those you are targeting. What's more, the regular use of pesticides can easily lead to the development of resistance.

The two most important things to remember are:
1. ALWAYS READ THE LABEL
2. NEVER USE PESTICIDES ON OR NEAR PLANTS THAT ARE IN FLOWER – INCLUDING WEEDS

All pesticides sold for garden use in the UK are rigorously tested and must be legally approved before they are marketed and passed as safe when used exactly according to the manufacturer's instructions. They are then issued with a MAPP number which you should always look for on the packaging.

FOR SAFETY
• Wear rubber gloves when using pesticides and wash your hands afterwards.
• If using a spray, protect your mouth and nose.
• Wash off any pesticide that comes in contact with your eyes and mouth immediately with plenty of cold water.
• Spray in the early morning or evening, not in the heat of the day or bright sunshine.
• Keep pesticides away from children and pets at all times. Keep containers locked away when not in use.
• Always replace caps after use and keep products in their original packaging.
• Never use pesticides anywhere near ponds or streams where they can damage or kill fish and amphibians.
• Select a pesticide carefully to make sure that it will target the creatures that are causing your problem.
• Never use more than the recommended dosage. It is better to apply a product little and often.
• Always avoid spraying on a windy day.
• If necessary, protect nearby plants before you spray, for example with sheets of plastic or cardboard.
• If spraying edible plants, check very carefully for any time interval necessary to avoid any deleterious effects.
• Spray thoroughly, taking care not to neglect leaf undersides.
• Dispose safely of any unwanted or out of date pesticides; take them to your recycling centre and declare their contents.

HOME-MADE PESTICIDES

Even if you have made them yourself, remember that these pesticides can still harm other creatures, your soil, or you yourself, so they should always be used with the general rules in mind.

Oil spray: mix 1 teaspoon each of liquid soap and vegetable oil, and mix with 1 litre of water. This works because when coated with oil the pores through which invertebrates breathe are blocked.

Soap spray: Dilute 1½ teaspoons of a mild liquid soap in 1 litre of water. This is particularly effective against aphids and beetles and works in the same way as the oil spray.

ORGANIC PESTICIDES

For a pesticide to be organic it must be made from plant or other natural substances. Compared with synthetic pesticides their effects are often short lived, so frequent applications are probably necessary. Because of their origins, organic treatments are safe to use on fruit, vegetables and other edible plants. These are the types most widely available commercially:

Pyrethrum and pyrethrins

The basis of these wide ranging insecticides are natural chemicals from the flowers of the Dalmatian chrysanthemum *Tanacetum cinerariifolium*. Available in spray or powder form it is active against aphids, thrips, ants and smaller caterpillars among others.

Fatty acids

Sold as insecticidal soap sprays, these will help to combat aphids, thrips, scale insects and spider mites.

Plant oils

Usually produced from sunflower or rapeseed oils, these sprays block the respiratory pores of aphids, thrips, scale insects, spider mites and the like. Their great advantage is that they are unlikely to damage bees, wasps and ladybirds. Neem oil, effective against aphids and a wide range of invertebrates is extracted from an Indian evergreen *Azadirachta indica.*

Garlic and seaweed extracts

These are usually offered as fumigants for the greenhouse to combat whitefly.

Slug pellets

Those marketed as safest to birds and mammals and approved by organic growers for use around edible and ornamental species contain ferric (iron) phosphate. The blue pellets are highly attractive to slugs and snails, which feed on them. The iron in the pellets blocks their throats and kills them by closing down their digestive systems.

WARNING!
SLUG PELLETS CONTAINING METALDEHYDE WERE WITHDRAWN IN 2020. DISPOSE SAFELY OF ANY YOU HAVE.

PLANT INVIGORATORS

Developed by tomato growers in Guernsey, these multi-functional products contain chemicals that aim to provide plants with optimal nutrition with the help of nitrogen, so maximizing their resistance to pests and diseases (notably fungal ones such as powdery mildew) combined with iron chelates, sticky soap-like compounds that adhere to insects and interfere with their respiration. Aphids, spider mites and scale insects are ideally treated with such mixtures, most of which are classed as organic. The treatment is given as a spray, easily bought ready mixed and needs to be applied on both upper and lower surfaces of leaves.

SYNTHETIC PESTICIDES

Non organic pesticides work in two main ways. They either kill on contact or are systemic, that is, they are absorbed by plant roots and leaves and become poisonous to any creature that eats them. Systemic compounds will also kill through contact.

Pyrethroids

Synthetic compounds based on, but enhancing, the basic chemistry of natural pyrethrum. They are generally least toxic to mammals but, because they are not super strong, need to be reapplied regularly. The most common chemical bases for these are:

Deltamethrin Marketed as a spray for treating a wide range of pests including aphids, caterpillars, codling moths, flea beetles, weevils, sawflies, scale insects and more. Safe to use on many fruits and vegetables.

Lambda-cyhalothrin Available as a concentrate which you can dilute yourself, or a ready-mixed spray. Safe on many fruits and vegetables, and will work effectively against aphids, beetles, caterpillars, sawflies, carrot flies and others.

Cypermethrin Buy as a spray or concentrate to dilute; will treat both ornamentals and edibles. It is particularly effective against aphids and can be bought mixed with a fungicide to help control both aphids and fungal diseases such as blackspot in one treatment.

Permethrin Usually comes as a smoke to treat insects such as aphids in greenhouses.

Acetamiprid A broad action spray-on treatment that will treat all kinds of insects including lily beetles and a range of caterpillars. Not all formulations are safe to use on fruit and vegetables, and even then the range will probably only include tomatoes, lettuce, potatoes, apples, pears and plums so check extra carefully before you use

them. It is sold in a mix with fungicides for treating downy mildew, blackspot, rust and similar conditions, specifically affecting roses.

Acetamiprid is also the key ingredient in compost drenches sold specifically for the treatment of vine weevils.

SYSTEMIC PRODUCTS
NOTE: INSECTICIDES CONTAINING IMIDACLOPRID AND THIAMETHOXAM ARE NOW PERMANENTLY BANNED. IF YOU STILL HAVE ANY PRODUCTS CONTAINING THESE CHEMICALS YOU SHOULD DISPOSE OF THEM SAFELY WITHOUT DELAY AT YOUR LOCAL RECYCLING CENTRE.

WILDLIFE AND THE LAW

However unwelcome some visitors to your garden may be, it is important to be aware of your legal obligations should you want to get rid of them. If you have doubts or questions, always contact your local authority or DEFRA (The Department for the Environment, Food and Rural Affairs).

In England, Wales and Scotland the primary legislation concerning animals, plants and habitats is The Wildlife & Countryside Act of 1981. As well as giving protection to native species, especially those under threat, it controls the release of non-native species into the wild and prohibits the use of certain types of snare. The penalty for breaking the law can be a fine of up to £50,000 or imprisonment.

Protection for animals is also provided by the Natural Environment and Rural Communities Act (2006) which singles out species of 'principal importance for the purpose of conserving biodiversity' which must be given priority treatment and confers on public bodies a 'duty of responsibility'. Creatures ranging from hedgehogs to newts are covered by this legislation.

Certain groups of animals are also covered by specific legislation. The Wild Mammals (Protection) Act of 1996, protects all mammals from mutilation of any kind. Any person who attacks an animal 'with intent to inflict unnecessary suffering' is deemed guilty of an offence.

For animals that you regard as pests – defined in law as 'insects or animals causing harm or nuisance to your property' – you can get help from your local authority or a certified pest controller. Rats and mice qualify as pests in this definition. However you must obey these rules:
• Only trap or kill permitted animals by legal methods.
• Only use poison specifically formulated for the creature in question.
• Only use approved traps.
• You may not use self-locking snares, bows or crossbows, explosives (except where legal in firearms), or use birds or other live creatures as decoys.

BADGERS

All badgers and their setts are protected under the Protection of Badgers Act 1992, so it is illegal to poison or kill them. This includes allowing your dog to kill a badger. If you want to make changes to your garden landscape that would involve disturbing a badger sett in any way, you need to obtain a special licence to do so from your local planning authority. The law would even apply if, by blocking off a badger's path into and out of your garden, you were denying it access to its sett. Deterring badgers with electric fencing or ultrasound is within the law, but there are no chemical deterrents yet approved for use.

FOXES

The law protects foxes from being killed with poison bait, with a self-locking snare or with a bow or crossbow. It is illegal to destroy, block or fill up a fox earth containing live foxes. Before using any manufactured scent-based fox repellent such as Renardine, check the Control of Pesticide Regulations (1986) and its various amendments. If you have trouble with foxes in your garden the best solution is to consult your local authority.

MOLES

Although moles have general protection under the 1996 Act, they can be treated as pests.

HEDGEHOGS

While offered general protection, hedgehogs are regarded as a species 'of principal importance' in the NERC Act (see left).

DEER

In order to protect deer (except for muntjac, which breed all year round) the law states that it is illegal to kill deer outside specific close seasons. You can check dates with The British Deer Society and request help from them in solving garden deer problems. All the pertinent gun regulations and licences apply to culling deer.

GREY SQUIRRELS

While it is legal to kill grey squirrels, which are regarded as pests, all the restrictions on humane treatment apply. However, because grey squirrels are classed as an Invasive Alien Species it is illegal to trap them, then release them into the wild.

RABBITS

If rabbits are a pest on your property they can be caught as long as you obey the law. However it is illegal to allow rabbits to escape from your property and cause damage to crops on any adjacent farmland.

AMPHIBIANS AND REPTILES

These creatures are given some protection in law. In addition to the general restrictions against killing and injuring, the 1981 Act deems it illegal to trade in our native species, including garden frogs, toads, newts, lizards, slow worms and adders.

BIRDS

All birds, their nests and eggs are legally protected, making it an offence, with certain exceptions, to: 'Intentionally kill, injure or take any wild bird. Intentionally take, damage or destroy the nest of any wild bird while it is in use or being built.'

To kill or take the eggs of 'nuisance' birds you must apply to DEFRA for a licence. It is only legal to kill or injure a wild bird if you can prove that your action is 'necessary to preserve public health or air safety, prevent spread of disease, or prevent serious damage to livestock, crops, vegetables, fruit, growing timber, or fisheries.' You will also be breaking the law if you transport wild birds, or their eggs, away from their natural habitats.

It is legal to take and care for an injured wild bird if your sole purpose is to tend it and then release it when it is no longer disabled. And a wild bird may be killed if it is beyond recovery. Licences for the shooting of birds are granted by Natural England. Controversially, since April 2019 such a licence has become obligatory for getting rid of pigeons, crows, gulls or any other birds you consider to be pests. Granting one is always likely to be considered a last resort.

PLANTS FOR WILDLIFE

From the hundreds of plants and flowers that will benefit wildlife in all seasons of the year, this is a very small selection intended to inspire and inform your garden planning and planting. Most are available in a range of varieties and cultivars, but remember that for pollinators, simple, accessible flowers are best, as are those with strong scents.

KEY TO FLOWERING TIMES
W: Winter, SP: Spring,
S: Summer, A: Autumn

Shrubs, climbers and small trees
Plants that provide garden structure plus, in most instances, beneficial flowers and fruit which are good food for birds.

(SP) Apples, plums, cherries and other *Prunus* species; many bear fruit
(S) Buddleja *Buddleia davidii* both the 'wild' type and cultivars such as 'Black Knight'
(SP) Cornelian cherry *Cornus mas*; also autumn fruit
(W) Spurge laurel *Daphne laureola*; also berries

(SP) Elder *Sambucus nigra*; autumn fruit
(SP) Flowering currant *Ribes sanguineum*
(SP) Hawthorn *Crataegus monogyna*; autumn fruit
(SP) Holly *Ilex aquifolium*; winter berries, but on female plants only
(S) Honeysuckle *Lonicera periclymenum*
(A/W) Ivy *Hedera helix*; valuable winter fruit
(SP) *Pyracantha* many varieties; useful fruit
(SP/S) Roses, native species; the dog rose *Rosa canina*, and field rose *Rosa arvensis*; fruit can last well into winter
(SP/S) Rowan *Sorbus aucuparia*; useful fruit
(W) *Viburnum* x *bodnantense*

Bulbs, corms and tubers
Many of these are vital in providing pollen and nectar in the winter and early spring for bumblebees and the like.

(SP and S) *Allium*; a variety of species in different seasons
(A) Autumn crocus *Colchicum* species
(W/SP) *Crocus* species; winter and spring flowering
(SP) Daffodils of which the best is *Narcissus pseudonarcissus* subsp *pseudonarcissus*
(S/A) Dahlia; single-flowered cultivars such as 'The Bishop of Llandaff'

(SP) Grape hyacinth *Muscari armeniacum*
(W) Hellebore *Helleborus* x *hybridus*
(SP) *Scilla siberica*
(W) Snowdrops *Galanthus nivalis* and *elwesii*
(SP) Star of Bethlehem *Ornithogalum umbellatum*

Herbs
Attractive through their scent as well as their pollen and nectar – and useful in the kitchen. Be sure to avoid non-flowering varieties and cultivars.

(S) Angelica *Angelica gigas* and other species
(S) Borage *Borago officinalis*
(SP) Chives *Allium schoenoprasum* and its varieties, including garlic chives
(S) Fennel *Foeniculum vulgare* and purple-leaved varieties; autumn seeds
(S) Oregano *Origanum laevigatum* and marjoram *O. majorana*
(SP/S) Rosemary *Rosmarinus* varieties and cultivars
(S) Sage *Salvia officinalis*, including purple-leaved types
(S) Spearmint *Mentha spicata* and its varieties
(S) Thyme *Thymus* varieties and cultivars

Perennials
From the massive number of species and varieties available, these are some that will always earn their place in a wildlife friendly garden.

(SP) Candytuft *Iberis sempervirens*
(S) Catmint *Nepeta grandiflora*
(S) Coneflower *Rudbeckia triloba*
(SP) Cowslip *Primula veris*
(SP/S) Cranesbill *Geranium pratense* and its cultivars, including early-flowering *G. phaeum*
(SP) Dame's violet *Hesperis matronalis*
(SP/S) Deadnettle *Lamium* species such as *orvala*
(S) Dyer's chamomile *Anthemis tinctoria*
(S) English lavender *Lavandula angustifolia*
(SP) Euphorbia *Euphorbia palustris* and many others
(S/A) Golden rod *Solidago rugosa*
(W/SP) Hellebore *Helleborus* species

and varieties

(S) Hemp agrimony *Eupatorium cannabinum*

(SP) Lungwort *Pulmonaria* cultivars such as 'Leopard', 'Ankum' and 'Diana Clare'

(S) Masterwort *Astrantia major*

(A) Michaelmas daisies *Aster novae-belgii* and its many cultivars

(S) Musk mallow *Malva moschata*

(S/A) *Penstemon* cultivars and varieties

(S) Perennial sweet pea *Lathyrus latifolius*

(SP/S/A) Perennial wallflower *Erysimum* species and cultivars, including biennials

(S) Garden phlox *Phlox paniculata*

(SP) Primrose *Primula vulgaris*

(S) Red valerian *Centranthus ruber*

(S) Scabious *Scabiosa columbaria*

(S) Sea holly *Eryngium* species and varieties

(S/A) Sedums such as *Sedum telephium* and *S.* 'Herbstfreude'

(SP/S) Speedwell *Veronica spicata*

(SP/S) Thrift *Armeria maritima*

(S) Valerian *Valeriana officinalis*

(S/A) *Verbena bonariensis*

(S) Yellow foxglove *Digitalis lutea*

Annuals and Biennials

Plants that not only brighten the garden but attract a great many pollinators and other creatures.

(SP/S) Alkanet *Anchusa azurea* and other species

(S) Coneflower *Rudbeckia* species

(S) Cornflower *Centaurea cyanus* – also some perennial varieties

(S/A) Evening primrose *Oenothera biennis*

(S) Foxglove *Digitalis* species and varieties. Also some perennials.

(S) French marigold *Tagetes patula*

(SP/S) Love-in-a-mist *Nigella damascena*

(S) Marigold *Calendula officinalis*

(S) Nasturtium *Tropaeolum majus*

(S) Poached egg plant *Limnanthes douglasii*

(S) Poppy *Papaver rhoeas*

(S/A) Sunflower *Helianthus annuus* – be sure to avoid pollen-free varieties. Excellent seedheads in autumn

(S) Sweet alyssum *Lobularia maritima*

(S/A) Tobacco plant *Nicotiana alata* evening scent.

INDEX